Drugs used in the treatment of mental health disorders:
Frequently
Asked
Questions
4th edition

...M
...RSITIES
AT
MEDWAY
LIBRARY

D1140389

MWCGH
08007380

8010851

Drugs used in the treatment of mental health disorders:
Frequently
Asked
Question**s**
4th edition

Edited by
Stephen Bazire

UNIVERSITIES AT MEDWAY LIBRARY

WITHDRAWN FROM UNIVERSITIES AT MEDWAY LIBRARY

APS Publishing, The Old School, Tollard Royal, Salisbury, Wiltshire, SP5 5PW
www.apspublishing.co.uk

British Library Cataloguing in Publication Data
A catalogue record for this book is available from the British Library

© Stephen Bazire and Norfolk Mental Health Care NHS Trust 2004
ISBN 1 9038772 7 X

All rights reserved. No part of this publication may be reproduced, stored in a retrieval system, or transmitted in any form or by any means, electronic, mechanical, photocopying, recording, or otherwise without prior permission from the publisher.
Printed in the UK by HSW Print, Tonypandy, Rhondda

Contents

Introduction

This book was initially written by Sarah Branch, BSc(Pharm), MRPharmS, DipComPharm, MPSI, as her pre-registration pharmacy project, with help from Stephen Bazire and the pharmacy staff at Hellesdon Hospital, and the co-operation and help of staff and relatives of patients of Norfolk Mental Health Care NHS Trust; it has been updated regularly and continuously.

The book sets out to answer the most common questions asked by patients, relatives, and carers, the list being compiled after an extensive survey of over 100 people. The aim is to have the book widely available and accessible, and to help stimulate interest and discussion on drug therapies for psychiatric illnesses. As well as direct information for clients or patients, its other uses will include use as a training and support package for carers and professionals. If you would like further information on any of these drugs or drug-related advice, please contact your local mental health pharmacy service.

Information in this book is based on published data. References include the UK British National Formulary (BNF, published by the British Medical Association and Royal Pharmaceutical Society of Great Britain), Martindale (the Extra Pharmacopoeia, published by RPSGB Pharmaceutical Press), Psychotropic Drug Directory 2003/4, SPCs (UK Manufacturers Summary of Product Characteristics, published by the Association of British Pharmaceutical Industry), MicroMedex (an independent and extensive CDROM-based drug information source), UK Psychiatric Pharmacy Group leaflets (www.ukppg.org.uk), Royal College of Psychiatrists advice and guidelines and the current medical literature.

The UK Psychiatric Pharmacy Group National Mental Health Medicines Telephone Helpline, hosted by the Maudsley Hospital and funded by NIMHE, UK, is available on 020-7919-2999 from 11am to 5pm, Monday to Friday.

Stephen Bazire BPharm, MRPharmS, DipPsychPharm, MCMHP
Pharmacy, Hellesdon Hospital
Norwich, NR6 5BE
United Kingdom
www.nmhct.nhs.uk/pharmacy
Declarations of interest on www.ukppg.org.uk/committee.html

Treatments for the symptoms of Alzheimer's disease

Drugs known as anticholinesterases

Drugs: Donepezil, galantamine and rivastigmine

Drugs available	Brand name(s)	Forms available			
		Tablets	Capsules	Liquid	Injection
Donepezil	Aricept®	✔			
Galantamine	Reminyl	✔		✔	
Rivastigmine	Exelon®		✔	✔	

Memantine (Ebixa®) is also for Alzheimer's Disease and is available in the UK but has a different action.

What are anticholinesterases used for?

Alzheimer's disease is an illness where the main symptoms are loss of memory, lack of social functioning, and personality changes. Anticholinesterases help to treat the symptoms of mild or moderate Alzheimer's disease. They do not help if the symptoms have become more severe. Studies so far have shown that around 60–80% of sufferers have either slightly improved or stabilised over six months.

How do anticholinesterases work?

The brain has chemical messengers that help to pass messages from one brain cell to another. One of these chemical messengers is called acetylcholine. It is involved in the areas of the brain that control learning and memory (e.g. remembering things and 'laying down' of memory). In Alzheimer's disease, there are many changes within the brain, but the main effect is of reduced acetylcholine activity. If you have less acetylcholine, you have less memory ability, reduced learning, etc.

Acetylcholine is broken down in the brain by an enzyme called acetylcholinesterase. These drugs block this enzyme and stop it breaking down acetylcholine. This increases the amount of acetylcholine and makes it last longer and, in turn, helps to stabilise or improve memory, learning, and functioning.

These drugs do not cure the condition, but in some people may improve the symptoms for a while. They probably do not slow the underlying decline.

How should I take it?

The tablets should be swallowed with at least half a glass of water while sitting or standing. This is to make sure that they reach the stomach and do not stick in the throat.

When should I take my drug?

Take your medication as directed on the medicine label. Try to take it at a regular time each day. If the label says take once a day, take it in the evening, just before going to bed.

How long do anticholinesterases take to work?

These drugs take about four weeks to show their full effect at the starting dose. After about four to eight weeks, your doctor may increase your dose.

For how long will I need to keep taking it?

This should be discussed with your doctor, as people's responses are different.

Are anticholinesterases addictive?

These drugs are not addictive. There is no evidence of withdrawal symptoms.

Can I stop taking anticholinesterases suddenly?

There are no known problems.

What sort of side-effects might occur?

Side-effect	What happens	What to do about it
Common		
Headache	When your head is painful and pounding	Ask your pharmacist if it is safe to take aspirin or paracetamol with any other drugs you may be taking
Loss of appetite	Not feeling hungry. You may lose weight	If this is a problem, contact your doctor or pharmacist for advice
Dizziness	Feeling light-headed and faint	Do not stand up too quickly. Try and lie or sit down if you feel it coming on. A change in dose may help. Discuss this with your doctor
Nausea and vomiting	Feeling sick and being sick	If it is severe, contact your doctor. It may be possible to adjust your dose
Diarrhoea	Going to the toilet more than usual and passing loose, watery stools	Drink plenty of water. If it lasts for more than a day, contact your doctor or pharmacist
Sleep disturbances	You cannot sleep very well and may have nightmares	If you feel like this for more than a week after starting the drug, tell your doctor
Uncommon		
Urinary retention	Not much urine is passed	Contact your doctor now
Rare		
Seizures	Having a fit or convulsion	Stop taking the drug and contact your doctor immediately.

Table adapted from UK Psychiatric Pharmacy Group leaflets, with kind permission (www.ukppg.org.uk)

Do not worry about this list of side-effects. You may not experience any. There are other rare side-effects. If you develop any unusual symptoms, ask your doctor about these at your next appointment.

What should I do if I forget to take a dose?

Start again as soon as you remember unless it is almost time for your next dose. Do not try to catch up by taking two or more doses at once, as you may experience more side-effects. If you miss several doses, start again when you remember. Tell your doctor about this at your next appointment.

Will an anticholinesterase make me drowsy?

Drowsiness is not a main side-effect of these drugs, but if you do feel drowsy, you should not drive (see below) or operate machinery. You should take extra care as they may affect your reaction times.

Will anticholinesterases cause weight gain?

Weight gain is not a common reported side-effect of donepezil nor galantamine, although it can sometimes happen with rivastigmine. If, however, you do start to have problems with your weight, tell your doctor at your next appointment, as he/she can arrange for you to see a dietician for advice.

Will an anticholinesterase affect my sex life?

These drugs are not thought to cause sexual problems.

Can I drink alcohol while I am taking an anticholinesterase?

There are no known problems.

Are there any foods or drinks that I should avoid?

You should have no problems with any food or drink.

Will anticholinesterases affect my other medication?

You should have no problems if you take other medications, although a few problems might occur with other drugs that affect the same part of the brain and possibly with some drugs for arthritis (such as NSAIDs).

If I am taking a contraceptive pill, will this be affected?

It is not thought that the contraceptive pill is affected by these drugs.

What if I want to start a family or discover I'm pregnant?

It is important to consider that there will be a risk to you and your child from taking a medicine during pregnancy, but also a possible risk from stopping the medicine, e.g. becoming ill again. Unfortunately, no decision is risk-free. It will be for you to decide which is the least risk. All we can do here is to help you understand some of the issues, so you can make an informed decision. For your information, major malformations occur 'spontaneously' in about 2–4% of all pregnancies, even if no drugs are taken. The main problem with medicines is termed 'teratogenicity, i.e. a medicine causing a malformation in the unborn child. A medicine causing teratogenicity is called a 'teratogen'. Since a baby has completed its main development between days 17 and 60 of the pregnancy (the so-called 'first trimester') these first 2–16 weeks are the main concern. After that, there may be other problems, e.g. some medicines may cause slower growth. The infant may also be affected after birth, e.g. withdrawal effects are possible with some drugs.

If possible, the best option is to plan in advance. If you think you could become pregnant, discuss this with your doctor and it may be possible to switch to medicines thought to carry least risk, and take other risk-reducing steps, e.g. adjusting doses, taking vitamin supplements, etc. If you have just discovered you are pregnant, don't panic, but seek advice from your GP within the next few days if possible. He or she may also want to refer you on to someone with more specialist knowledge of your medicine.

Very few medicines have been shown to be completely safe in pregnancy and so no manufacturer or advisor can ever say any medicine is safe. They will usually advise not to take a medicine during pregnancy, unless the benefit is much greater than the risk. In the UK, there is the NTIS (National Teratology Information Service) which offers individual risk assessments. However, this advice should always be used to help you and your doctor decide what is the risk to you and your baby. There is a risk from taking the medicine and a risk should you stop a medicine, e.g. you might become ill again and need to go back on the medication again. The advice offered here is just that, i.e. advice, but may give you some idea about the possible risks and what (at the time of writing) is known through the medical press.

It may be helpful to know that in the USA, the FDA (Federal Drug Administration) classifies medicines in pregnancy in five groups:

A =	Studies show no risk, so harm to the unborn child appears only a remote possibility
B =	Animal and human studies indicate a lack of risk, but are not fully conclusive
C =	Animal studies indicate a risk, but there is no safety data in humans
D =	A definite risk exists, but the benefit may outweigh the risk in some people
X =	The risk outweighs any possible benefit

Donepezil and rivastigmine are classified as 'C'. There is no evidence of a teratogenic effect, and animal tests show a low risk of danger, but you should still seek personal advice from your GP, who may then, if necessary, seek further specialist advice.

Will I need a blood test?

You should not need to have a blood test to check on your drug, although your doctor may want to check your blood for other reasons.

Can I drive while I am taking an anticholinesterase?

These drugs should not affect your ability to carry out skilled tasks, such as driving or operating machinery.

Treatments for anxiety

Drugs known as anxiolytics (often wrongly called the 'minor tranquillisers')

Drug group: Benzodiazepines

Drugs available	Brand name(s)	Forms available			
		Tablets	Capsules	Liquid	Injection
*Alprazolam	Xanax®	✔			
*Bromazepam	Lexotan®	✔			
Chlordiazepoxide	Librium® Tropium®	✔	✔		
*Clobazam	Frisium®		✔		
*Clonazepam	Rivotril®	✔			✔
*Clorazepate dipotassium	Tranxene®		✔		
Diazepam≠	Many brands≠	✔		✔	✔
Lorazepam	Ativan®	✔			✔
Oxazepam	Serenid®	✔			

*   means that these products are not available on the NHS for anxiety
≠   Diazepam is available as many 'branded generics' (e.g. Tensium®), as well as the better known Valium®. It is also available as suppositories and rectal tubules.

What are they used for?

The benzodiazepines are 'calmers'. They help to reduce excessive agitation and can make you sleepy. They are, therefore, used to help treat, but not cure symptoms of anxiety, such as tension, feeling shaky, sweating, and difficulty in thinking logically. They also have muscle-relaxing properties and some can be used to help epilepsy, e.g. clonazepam, and particularly 'status epilepticus', e.g. diazepam.

How do they work?

When you are anxious, your brain becomes more active. It may then produce a chemical messenger (or 'neurotransmitter') called GABA that makes you feel calmer. GABA is the brain's naturally occurring 'calmer'. The benzodiazepines make the action of GABA more powerful and this helps to calm the brain.

How should I take them?

Tablets and capsules:

Tablets and capsules should be swallowed with at least half a glass of water while sitting or standing. This is to ensure that they reach the stomach and do not stick in the throat.

Liquids:

Your pharmacist should give you a medicine spoon. Use it carefully to make sure you measure the correct amount. Ask your pharmacist for a medicine spoon, if you do not have one.

Shake the bottle well before use, as the drug can settle to the bottom and cause you to receive too low a dose at the start and too high a dose at the end of the bottle.

When should I take them?

Take your medication as directed on the medicine label. Try to take it at regular times each day. It may be easier to remember if you take it at meal times, as there is no problem about taking any of these drugs with or after food. If the instructions say to take the drugs **once** a day, this is usually best at bedtime, as they should make you drowsy and help you to sleep.

How long will they take to work?

They should begin to work soon after you start to take them. Later, your doctor may need to change the dose to suit you.

For how long will I need to keep taking them?

This should be discussed with your doctor, as people's responses are different. Benzodiazepines are very safe drugs if used sensibly. They are best taken in as low a dose as possible for a short time, e.g. as a 'first aid' measure. Usually, this should be no longer than one month to help you overcome your problems and for other treatments to start working. If you need to take them for longer, you should discuss this regularly with your doctor. Some people with long-term problems may need to take them for longer.

Are they addictive?

Due to the effects that benzodiazepines have on the brain, they can sometimes produce 'dependence' or 'addiction' if taken regularly every day for more than four to six weeks. Dependence or addiction means that you cannot manage without the drugs because if you stop taking them, you experience withdrawal symptoms. In the worst cases, withdrawal symptoms from the benzodiazepines could include: anxiety, tension, panic attacks, poor concentration, difficulty in sleeping, nausea, trembling, palpitations, sweating, and pains and stiffness in your face, head, and neck. These withdrawal symptoms could occur several days after stopping your benzodiazepine. They may last from one to three weeks, but can go on for months. If you have taken them for a long time, your doctor will need to take you off your benzodiazepine gradually. This will be done by reducing your dose slowly over a period of time to reduce the chance of withdrawal effects.

It is also true that many people suffer no withdrawal symptoms when they stop taking benzodiazepines, even if they have been taking them for many years. Some people also argue that the 'withdrawal' symptoms are almost exactly the same as the symptoms of anxiety, and are, in fact, the return of the original symptoms. You should make sure that you discuss your particular treatment with your doctor.

Can I stop taking them suddenly?

It is better not to stop taking them suddenly, if you have been taking them regularly every day for more than four to six weeks. If you do you may experience some of the withdrawal effects mentioned above. If you take them only when really necessary (e.g. for one or two weeks during a severe attack of anxiety, and then have several weeks without them) this is better than taking them all the time and can prevent you becoming dependent. You should talk to your doctor about this.

What should I do if I forget to take them?

Start again as soon as you remember unless it is almost time for your next dose. Do not try to catch up by taking two or more doses at once, as you may experience more side-effects, e.g. sleepiness. If you miss several doses, start again when you remember. Tell your doctor about this at your next appointment.

What sort of side-effects might occur?

Side-effect	What happens	What to do about it
Common		
Drowsiness	You feel sleepy or sluggish. It can last for a few hours after taking your dose or longer	Do not drive or use machinery. Discuss with your doctor if you can take your benzodiazepine at a different time of the day
Dizziness	Feeling light-headed and faint	Do not stand up too quickly. Try and lie or sit down if you feel it coming on. Do not drive
Less common		
Ataxia	Being unsteady on your feet.	Discuss with your doctor at your next appointment
Rare		
Aggression	Feeling excitable. You may be talkative, unfriendly, or disinhibited	Discuss this with your doctor who may want to adjust your drug or dose
Headache	Your head is pounding and painful	Try aspirin or paracetamol. Your pharmacist will be able to advise if these are safe to take with other drugs that you may be taking
Confusion	Your mind is all mixed up or confused	Discuss with your doctor who may want to adjust your drug or dose
Hypotension	Low blood pressure—this can make you feel dizzy, particularly when you stand up	It is not dangerous. Do not stand up too quickly. If you feel dizzy, do not drive
Amnesia	Loss of short-term memory or difficulty in remembering	It is not dangerous. Discuss with your doctor if you are worried.
Rashes	Blotches seen anywhere	Stop taking the drug and see your doctor now

Table adapted from UK Psychiatric Pharmacy Group leaflets, with kind permission (www.ukppg.org.uk)

Do not be worried by this list of side-effects, as you may not experience any. There are other rare side-effects. If you develop any unusual symptoms, ask your doctor about these at your next appointment.

Will they make me drowsy?

Depending on the dose, these drugs should help to calm you down, but they can calm you down too much and send you to sleep. They may make you feel a bit drowsy, even at a usual dose. If you are taking them at night, you may feel drowsy the next morning, so you should not drive (see below) or operate machinery until you know how they affect you. You should take extra care as these drugs may affect your reaction times.

Will they cause weight gain?

It is not thought that the benzodiazepines cause any changes in weight. If you do start to have problems with your weight, discuss these with your doctor at your next appointment, who can then arrange an appointment with a dietician for advice.

Will it affect my sex life?

Benzodiazepines do not have any known, significant effects. Drowsiness may have some effect. In some people reduced anxiety may be an advantage.

Can I drink alcohol while I am taking these drugs?

If you drink alcohol while taking these drugs, it may make you feel sleepier. This is particularly important if you need to drive or operate machinery, and you must seek advice on this. They may affect your reflexes or reaction times. They can also increase the effects of alcohol, so it is better to avoid alcohol.

Are there any foods or drinks that I should avoid?

You should have no problems with any food or drink other than alcohol (see above).

Will they affect my other medication?

You should have no problems if you take other medications, although a few can occur. Make sure your doctor knows about all the medicines you are taking. The benzodiazepines can 'interact' with other sleeping drugs and some antidepressants, by increasing their sedative effect, although your doctor should know about these. Some other medicines, e.g. the painkiller, co-proxamol ('Distalgesic®') can make you drowsy. When combined with your benzo-diazepines, this could make you even drowsier. This does not necessarily mean the drugs cannot be used together, just that you may need to follow your doctor's instructions very carefully. You should tell your doctor before starting or stopping these or any other drugs.

If I am taking a contraceptive pill, will this be affected?

It is not thought that the contraceptive pill is affected by any of these drugs.

What if I want to start a family or discover I'm pregnant?

It is important to consider that there will be a risk to you and your child from taking a medicine during pregnancy, but also a possible risk from stopping the medicine, e.g. becoming ill again. Unfortunately, no decision is risk-free. It will be for you to decide which is the least risk. All we can do here is to help you understand some of the issues, so you can make an informed decision. For your information, major malformations occur 'spontaneously' in about 2–4% of all pregnancies, even if no drugs are taken. The main problem with medicines is termed 'teratogenicity', i.e. a medicine causing a malformation in the unborn child. A medicine causing teratogenicity is called a 'teratogen'. Since a baby has completed its main development between days 17 and 60 of the pregnancy (the so-called 'first trimester') these first 2–16 weeks are the main concern. After that, there may be other problems, e.g. some medicines may cause slower growth. The infant may also be affected after birth, e.g. withdrawal effects are possible with some drugs.

If possible, the best option is to plan in advance. If you think you could become pregnant, discuss this with your doctor and it may be possible to switch to medicines thought to carry least risk, and take other risk-reducing steps, e.g. adjusting doses, taking vitamin supplements, etc. If you have just discovered you are pregnant, don't panic, but seek advice from your GP within the next few days if possible. He or she may also want to refer you on to someone with more specialist knowledge of your medicine.

Very few medicines have been shown to be completely safe in pregnancy and so no manufacturer or advisor can ever say any medicine is safe. They will usually advise not to take a medicine during pregnancy, unless the benefit is much greater than the risk. In the UK, there is the NTIS (National Teratology Information Service) which offers individual risk assessments. However, this advice should always be used to help you and your doctor decide what is the risk to you and your baby. There is a risk from taking the medicine and a risk should you stop a medicine, e.g. you might become ill again and need to go back on the medication. The advice offered here is just that, i.e. advice, but may give you some idea about the possible risks and what (at the time of writing) is known through the medical press.

It may be helpful to know that in the USA, the FDA (Federal Drug Administration) classifies medicines in pregnancy in five groups:

A =	Studies show no risk, so harm to the unborn child appears only a remote possibility
B =	Animal and human studies indicate a lack of risk, but are not fully conclusive
C =	Animal studies indicate a risk, but there is no safety data in humans
D =	A definite risk exists, but the benefit may outweigh the risk in some people
X =	The risk outweighs any possible benefit

The benzodiazepines are classified as follows:

- Alprazolam 'D'
- Chlordiazepoxide 'D'
- Clonazepam 'C'
- Diazepam 'D'
- Lorazepam 'D'
- Oxazepam 'D.

The others are not classified as they are not available in USA. Although some studies have shown a slightly increased chance of abnormalities with benzodiazepines, it is possible that alcohol and other drug use may have been the reason for this. The risk of oral clefts is reported to be about 7 in 1000 births with diazepam. Occasional use of shorter-acting benzodiazepines would appear to have a very low risk. Regular use of longer-acting benzodiazepines (e.g. chlordiazepoxide, diazepam) may also lead to some short-term breathing difficulties in newborn babies, and some withdrawal effects, e.g. the floppy baby syndrome. You should seek personal advice from your GP, who may then, if necessary, seek further specialist advice.

Will I need a blood test?

You will not need to have a blood test to check on your benzodiazepine.

Can I drive while I am taking them?

The benzodiazepines can reduce your ability to carry out skilled tasks, such as driving or operating machinery. You may also feel drowsy the day after you take them. Until these effects wear off, or you know how your drug affects you, do not drive or operate machinery. You should take extra care, as they may affect your reaction times.

It is an offence to drive, to attempt to drive, or to be in charge of a vehicle when unfit through drugs. It is advisable to let your insurance company know if you are taking these drugs. If you do not and you have an accident, it could affect your insurance cover.

If you are advised by your doctor not to drive, and continue to do so, the General Medical Council has advised doctors to inform the DVLA. The DVLA may then carry out an enquiry.

Drug group: Beta-blockers

Drugs available	Brand name(s)	Forms available			
		Tablets	Capsules	Liquid	Injection
Oxprenolol	Trasicor® Slow-Trasicor® Apsolox®	✔			
Propranolol	Inderal®, Inderal-LA®	✔	✔	✔	✔

Some other beta-blockers may have similar effects.

For what are beta-blockers used?

In lower dose, beta-blockers can be used to help treat the symptoms of anxiety, e.g. palpitations, sweating, or shakiness. They are more usually used to help heart conditions, such as hypertension (high blood pressure), angina, or irregular heartbeats (arrhythmias).

How do beta-blockers work for anxiety?

When you are anxious, your brain becomes more active and alert. It may then make more of the chemical messengers called noradrenaline and adrenaline. These will cause an increase in your heart rate and may make your body shake, sweat, etc, and increase feelings of anxiety. The beta-blockers reduce the effect of these transmitters, thereby reducing the physical symptoms of anxiety. There are other drug treatments for anxiety, e.g. the benzodiazepines (diazepam, etc).

How should I take them?

Tablets and capsules:

Tablets should be swallowed with at least half a glass of water while sitting or standing. **Capsules** should be swallowed **whole** with at least half a glass of water while sitting or standing. This is to ensure that both tablets or capsules reach the stomach and do not stick in the throat. The capsules are a 'sustained-release' preparation and should not be sucked or chewed.

Liquid:

Your pharmacist should give you a medicine spoon. Use it carefully to measure the correct amount. Ask your pharmacist for a medicine spoon if you do not have one. Shake the bottle well before use.

When should I take my beta-blockers?

Take your medication as directed on the medicine label. Try to take them at regular times each day. Taking them at meal times may make it easier to remember, as there is no problem about taking these drugs with or after food.

How long will the beta-blockers take to work?

They should start to work on your symptoms fairly soon after you begin taking them, e.g. within a few hours. Later, your doctor may need to alter the dose to suit you.

For how long will I need to keep taking them?

This should be discussed with your doctor as people's responses are different. The beta-blockers are best taken in a fairly low dose, as a 'first aid' measure.

Are the beta-blockers addictive?

The beta-blockers are not addictive. They only act on the physical symptoms of anxiety, although it is not advisable to stop taking them suddenly (see next question).

Can I stop taking beta-blockers suddenly?

It is not advisable to stop taking beta-blockers suddenly if you have been taking them regularly every day for more than four to six weeks, although there probably would be no major problem if you are only taking a low dose. A gradual reduction in your dose is better.

What should I do if I forget to take a dose?

Start again as soon as you remember unless it is almost time for your next dose. Do not try to catch up by taking two or more doses at once, as this may increase the risk of side-effects. If you miss several doses, start again when you remember. Tell your doctor about this at your next appointment.

Will the beta-blocker make me drowsy?

Some people do feel a little drowsy, particularly at the start of treatment, but this should wear off. If you do feel drowsy, you should not drive (see below) or operate machinery until you know how the drug affects you. You should take extra care, as it may affect your reaction times.

Will the beta-blocker cause weight gain?

It is not thought that the beta-blockers cause any great changes in weight, although it has been reported that a few people put on a small amount of weight over several years. If, however, you do start to have problems with your weight, tell your doctor at your next appointment, who can then arrange for you to see a dietician for advice about an appropriate diet.

What sort of side-effects might occur?

Side-effect	What happens	What to do about it
Common		
Fatigue	You feel tired all the time. This may happen early on in treatment and should go away	If you feel like this for more than a week after starting the beta-blocker, tell your doctor. It may be possible to adjust your dose slightly
Cold extremities	Your toes and fingers feel cold. This may happen early on in treatment and should go away	If you feel like this for more than a week after starting the beta-blocker, tell your doctor. It may be possible to adjust your dose slightly
Uncommon		
Stomach upset	This includes feeling sick and diarrhoea (the runs)	If you feel like this for more than a week after starting the beta-blocker, tell your doctor
Sleep disturbances	You cannot sleep very well and may have nightmares	If you feel like this for more than a week after starting the beta-blocker, tell your doctor
Dizziness	Feeling light-headed and faint, especially when you stand up	Do not stand up too quickly. Try and lie down when you feel it coming on. Do not drive. Let your doctor know at your next appointment
Wheeziness	Difficulty in breathing, and your chest feels tight	This may happen if you have asthma. Contact your doctor now
Bradycardia	A very slow pulse (under 50 beats per minute)	Contact your doctor now
Rare		
Skin trouble	For example, a rash or itching that you have not had before	Contact your doctor now
Dry eyes	Your eyes feel dry	Contact your doctor

Table adapted from UK Psychiatric Pharmacy Group leaflets, with kind permission (www.ukppg.org.uk)

Do not worry about this list of side-effects, as you may not experience any. There are other rare side-effects. If you develop any unusual symptoms, ask your doctor about these at your next appointment.

Will the beta-blocker affect my sex life?

Beta-blockers do not have any known significant effects. Higher doses may reduce blood pressure in some people (which is often why they are prescribed), and this may have a detrimental effect on some men's ability to achieve an erection. In some people, reduced anxiety may be an advantage.

Can I drink alcohol while I am taking a beta-blocker?

Alcohol may slightly reduce the effect of your beta-blocker, but this is unlikely to be a problem.

Are there any foods or drinks that I should avoid?

You should have no problems with any food or drink other than alcohol (see above).

Will the beta-blocker affect my other medication?

You should not have problems if you take other medications, but there are a few that can occur. Make sure your doctor knows about any other medicines you are taking, and that he/she knows about any heart, breathing, thyroid, or diabetic disorders you have had in the past. For example, you should not normally take a beta-blocker if you have asthma.

The beta-blockers can 'interact' with some other drugs, e.g. treatments for high blood pressure, glaucoma, and some antidepressants. This does not necessarily mean the drugs cannot be used together, just that you may need to follow your doctor's instructions very carefully. You should tell your doctor before starting or stopping these, or any other drugs.

If I am taking a contraceptive pill, will this be affected?

It is not thought that the contraceptive pill is affected by these drugs.

What if I want to start a family or discover I'm pregnant?

It is important to consider that there will be a risk to you and your child from taking a medicine during pregnancy, but also a possible risk from stopping the medicine, e.g. suffering from a relapse. Unfortunately, no decision is risk-free. It will be for you to decide which is the least risk. All we can do here is to help you understand some of the issues, so that you can make an informed decision. For your information, major malformations occur 'spontaneously' in about 2–4% of all pregnancies, even if no drugs are taken. The main problem with medicines is termed 'teratogenicity', i.e. a medicine causing a malformation in the unborn child. A medicine causing teratogenicity is called a 'teratogen'. Since a baby has completed it's main development between days 17 and 60 of the pregnancy (the so-called 'first trimester') these first 2–16 weeks are the main concern. After that, there may be other problems, e.g. some medicines may cause slower growth. The infant may also be affected after birth, e.g. withdrawal effects are possible with some drugs.

If possible, the best option is to plan in advance. If you think you could become pregnant, discuss this with your doctor and it may be possible to switch to medicines thought to carry least risk, and take other risk-reducing steps, e.g. adjusting doses, taking vitamin supplements, etc. If you have just discovered you are pregnant, don't panic, but seek advice from your GP within the next few days if possible. He or she may also want to refer you on to someone with more specialist knowledge of your medicine.

Very few medicines have been shown to be completely safe in pregnancy and so no manufacturer or advisor can ever say any medicine is safe. They will usually advise not to take a medicine during pregnancy, unless the benefit is much greater than the risk. In the UK, there is the NTIS (National Teratology Information Service) who offer individual risk assessments. However, their advice should always be used to help you and your doctor decide what is the risk to you and your baby. There is a risk from taking the medicine and a risk should you stop a medicine, e.g. you might become ill again and need to go back on the medication again. The advice offered here is just that—advice, but may give you some idea about the possible risks and what (at the time of writing) is known through the medical press.

It may be helpful to know that in the USA, the FDA (Federal Drug Administration) classifies medicines in pregnancy in five groups:

A =	Studies show no risk, so harm to the unborn child appears only a remote possibility
B =	Animal and human studies indicate a lack of risk, but are not fully conclusive
C =	Animal studies indicate a risk, but there is no safety data in humans
D =	A definite risk exists, but the benefit may outweigh the risk in some people
X =	The risk outweighs any possible benefit

The beta-blockers propranolol and oxprenolol are classified as 'C'. There is no proven evidence of a teratogenic effect, and animal tests show a low risk of danger. Some problems have been reported, especially later in pregnancy, and so you should seek personal advice from your GP, who may then, if necessary, seek further specialist advice. Reducing your dose a few weeks before your due date may also be possible.

Will I need a blood test?

You should not need to have a blood test to check on your beta-blocker, although your doctor may want to check your blood for other reasons.

Can I drive while I am taking a beta-blocker?

The beta-blockers can reduce your ability to carry out skilled tasks, such as driving or operating machinery. You may also feel drowsy when you start to take them. Until these effects wear off, or you know how your drug affects you, do not drive or operate machinery. You should take extra care, as they may affect your reaction times.

It is an offence to drive, to attempt to drive, or to be in charge of a vehicle when unfit through drugs. It is a advisable to let your insurance company know if you are taking these drugs. If you do not and you have an accident, it could affect your insurance cover.

If you are advised by your doctor not to drive, and continue to do so, the General Medical Council has advised doctors to inform the DVLA. The DVLA may then carry out an enquiry.

Drug: Buspirone

Drug	Brand name	Forms available			
		Tablets	**Capsules**	**Liquid**	**Injection**
Buspirone	Buspar®	✔			

For what is buspirone used?

Buspirone is used to help treat anxiety. It is quite different to the benzodiazepines (e.g. diazepam).

How does buspirone work?

It is not entirely clear how buspirone works. It probably works by having an effect on serotonin (5-HT) receptors in the brain. It is not, however, a sedative.

How should I take buspirone?

The tablet(s) should be swallowed with at least half a glass of water while sitting or standing. This is to make sure that they reach the stomach and do not stick in the throat.

When should I take buspirone?

Take your medication as directed on the medicine label. Try to take it at regular times each day. It may be easier to remember to take it at meal times, as there is no problem about taking buspirone with or after food.

How long will buspirone take to work?

Buspirone may take up to four weeks at full dosage to have an effect (ie, 10mg three times a day). This is longer than many other anxiolytic drugs, so do not give up too soon.

For how long will I need to keep taking buspirone?

This should be discussed with your doctor as people's responses are different. It is quite possible that you may need to take the drug for a long time.

Is buspirone addictive?

There have been no reports of addiction or dependence to buspirone.

Can I stop taking buspirone suddenly?

Although buspirone is not addictive, it is always advisable with any drug to gradually reduce the dosage. You should talk about this with your doctor.

What should I do if I forget to take a dose?

Start again as soon as you remember, unless it is almost time for your next dose. Do not try to catch up by taking two or more doses at once, as this may increase the risk of side-effects. If you miss several doses, start again when you remember. Tell your doctor about this at your next appointment.

Will buspirone make me drowsy?

Buspirone does not usually cause drowsiness.

Will buspirone cause weight gain?

Buspirone is not thought to cause any changes to weight. Should you experience problems with your weight, tell your doctor at your next appointment who can then arrange for you to see a dietician for advice.

What sort of side-effects might occur?

Side-effect	What happens	What to do about it
Common		
Headache	Your head is pounding and painful	Try aspirin or paracetamol. Your pharmacist will be able to advise if these are safe to take with other drugs you may be taking
Anxiety	Feeling more tense, nervous, or excitable	This should wear off. If not, mention it to your doctor at your next appointment
Nausea	Feeling sick	If it is severe, contact your doctor
Dizziness	Feeling light-headed and faint	Do not stand up too quickly. Try and lie or sit down if you start feeling dizzy. Do not drive
Less common		
Drowsiness	You feel sleepy or sluggish. It can last for a few hours or longer after taking your dose	Do not drive or use machinery. Discuss with your doctor whether you can take your buspirone at a different time of the day
Rare		
Tachycardia or palpitations	A rapid heart beat	See your doctor. It can be treated if it lasts for a long time
Fatigue	You feel tired all the time. This may happen early on in treatment and should go away	If you feel like this for more than a week after starting the drug, tell your doctor. It may be possible to adjust your dose slightly
Sweating	Feeling hot and sticky. Your clothes may be wet	Contact your doctor. You will need to have your blood pressure checked
Confusion	Your mind is all mixed up or confused	Discuss with your doctor at your next appointment. He/she may then want to adjust your drug or dose

Table adapted from UK Psychiatric Pharmacy Group leaflets, with kind permission (www.ukppg.org.uk)

Do not worry about this list of side-effects, as you may not experience any. There are other rare side-effects. If you develop any unusual symptoms, ask your doctor about these at your next appointment.

Will buspirone affect my sex life?

Buspirone is not thought to have any known significant effects on people's sex lives. In some people, reduced anxiety may be an advantage.

Can I drink alcohol while I am taking buspirone?

It is not thought that alcohol in moderation is a problem with buspirone, although some people may feel slightly unwell with this combination.

Are there any foods or drinks that I should avoid?

You should have no problems with any food or drink, although if you drink several litres of concentrated grapefruit juice, you could suffer more buspirone side-effects.

Will buspirone affect my other medication?

You should not have any problems if you take other medications, but a few problems can occur. Make sure your doctor knows about all the medicines you are taking. Buspirone can 'interact' with some antibiotics, e.g., erythromycin, itraconazole, and rifampicin. This is not dangerous, but you may experience more side-effects from your buspirone. It should not be taken with MAOI antidepressants.

If I am taking a contraceptive pill, will this be affected?

It is not thought that the contraceptive pill is affected by buspirone.

What if I want to start a family or discover I'm pregnant?

It is important to consider that there will be a risk to you and your child from taking a medicine during pregnancy, but also a possible risk from stopping the medicine, e.g., suffering a relapse. Unfortunately, no decision is risk-free. It will be for you to decide which is the least risk. All we can do here is to help you understand some of the issues, so you can make an informed decision. For your information, major malformations occur 'spontaneously' in about 2–4% of all pregnancies, even if no drugs are taken. The main problem with medicines is termed 'teratogenicity', i.e. a medicine causing a malformation in the unborn child. A medicine causing teratogenicity is called a 'teratogen'. Since a baby has completed its main development between days 17 and 60 of the pregnancy (the so-called 'first trimester'), these first 2–16 weeks are the main concern. After that, there may be other problems, e.g. some medicines may cause slower growth. The infant may also be affected after birth, e.g. withdrawal effects are possible with some drugs.

If possible, the best option is to plan in advance. If you think you could become pregnant, discuss this with your doctor and it may be possible to switch to medicines thought to carry least risk, and take other risk-reducing steps, e.g. adjusting doses, taking vitamin supplements, etc. If you have just discovered you are pregnant, don't panic, but, if possible, seek advice from your GP within the next few days. He or she may also want to refer you on to someone with more specialist knowledge of your medicine.

Very few medicines have been shown to be completely safe in pregnancy, so no manufacturer or advisor can ever say any medicine is safe. They will usually advise not to take a medicine during pregnancy unless the benefit is much greater than the risk. In the UK, there is the NTIS (National Teratology Information Service) who offer individual risk assessments. However, their advice should always be used to help you and your doctor decide what is the risk to you and your baby. There is a risk from taking the medicine and a risk should you stop a medicine, e.g. you might become ill again and need to go back on the medication. The advice offered here is just that—advice, but may give you some idea about the possible risks and what (at the time of writing) is known through the medical press.

It may be helpful to know that in the USA, the FDA (Federal Drug Administration) classifies medicines in pregnancy in five groups:

A =	Studies show no risk, so harm to the unborn child appears only a remote possibility
B =	Animal and human studies indicate a lack of risk, but are not fully conclusive
C =	Animal studies indicate a risk, but there is no safety date in humans
D =	A definite risk exists, but the benefit may outweigh the risk in some people
X =	The risk outweighs any possible benefit

Buspirone is classified as 'B'. There is no evidence of a teratogenic effect, animal tests show a low risk of danger, but you should still seek personal advice from your GP, who may then if necessary seek further specialist advice.

Will I need a blood test?

You will not need to have a blood test to check on your buspirone.

Can I drive while I am taking buspirone?

Although unlikely, buspirone can reduce your ability to carry out skilled tasks, such as driving or operating machinery. Until you know how your drug affects you, do not drive or operate machinery. You should take extra care, as it may affect your reaction times.

It is an offence to drive, to attempt to drive, or to be in charge of a vehicle when unfit through drugs.

Treatments for depression

Drugs known as antidepressants

Drug group: *Tricyclic antidepressants*

Drugs available	Brand name(s)	Forms available			
		Tablets	Capsules	Liquid	Injection
Amitriptyline	Tryptizol®	✔		✔	
Amoxapine[2]	Asendis®	✔			
Clomipramine	Anafranil®	✔	✔		
Dothiepin or dosulepin [1]	Prothiaden®	✔	✔	✔	
Doxepin	Sinequan®		✔		
Imipramine	Tofranil®	✔			
Lofepramine	Gamanil®	✔		✔	
Maprotiline	Ludiomil®	✔			
Nortriptyline	Allegron®	✔			
Trimipramine	Surmontil®	✔	✔		

'Motipress®' and 'Motival®' contain a small amount of nortriptyline and fluphenazine.
1. Dothiepin changed its name to dosulepin in 1998, although both are still in use.
2. Amoxapine is being discontinued in 2004/5.

What are the tricyclics used for?

Tricyclics are used to improve mood in people who are feeling low or depressed. The tricyclics may also be used to help the symptoms of anxiety and a number of other disorders. The tricyclics are among the most commonly prescribed antidepressants, but there are many others. All these drugs seem to be equally effective at the proper dose, but have different side-effects. If one drug does not suit you, it may be possible to try another.

How do the tricyclics work?

The brain has many naturally occurring chemical messengers. Two of these are called serotonin (sometimes called 5-HT) and noradrenaline. Both are important in the areas of the brain that control or regulate mood and thinking. It is known that these two chemical messengers are not as effective or active as normal in in the brain of someone who is depressed. Tricyclic antidepressants increase the amount of these chemical messengers, thus helping to correct the lack of action of the messengers and improving mood. The tricyclics can also effect other chemicals in the brain, e.g. 'acetylcholine', and this is the cause of some of their side-effects.

How should I take them ?

Tablets and capsules:

Tablets and capsules should be swallowed with at least half a glass of water while sitting or standing. This is to ensure that they reach the stomach and do not stick in the throat.

'Anafranil S/R®' (modified release) tablets should be swallowed whole and not chewed. This is because these tablets are made so that they release the drug over a longer period of time. This can help to reduce side-effects, or reduce the number of times a day you need to take your medicine. Crushing or chewing the tablets will cause the drug to be released too quickly and increase the risk of side-effects.

Liquids:

Your pharmacist should give you a medicine spoon or an oral syringe. Use it carefully to measure the correct amount. Ask your pharmacist for a medicine spoon if you do not have one. Shake the bottle well before use, as the drug can settle to the bottom; thus a dose at the start of the bottle could be too low, while a dose at the end could be too high. Your mouth may feel a little numb after taking one of these liquids, as they can have a local anaesthetic effect. This is common and nothing to worry about.

When should I take my tricyclic?

Take your medication as directed on the medicine label. Try to take it at regular times each day. Taking it at mealtimes may make dose times easier to remember, and there is no problem about taking any of these drugs with or after food. If the instructions say to take them **once** a day, this is usually better at bedtime, as they may make you drowsy when you first start taking them. However, they are not sleeping tablets as such.

How long will the tricyclics take to work?

It may then take two weeks or more before the tricyclics start to have any effect on your mood, and a further three or four weeks for this effect to reach its maximum. If it has not started working after about six weeks, it is unlikely to work. Unfortunately, in some people, the effect may take a little longer to occur, e.g. several months if you are older.

For how long will I need to keep taking the tricyclic?

This should be discussed with your doctor, as people's responses are different. To help you make a decision, it may be useful for you to know that research has shown that:

- for a first episode of major depression, your chances of becoming depressed again are much lower if you keep taking the antidepressant for six months after you have recovered (longer if you have risk factors for becoming depressed again)
- for a second episode, your chances of becoming depressed again are lower if you keep taking the antidepressant for one or two years after you have recovered
- for depression that keeps returning, continuing to take an antidepressant has been shown to have a protective effect for at least five years.

Are the tricyclics addictive?

They are not addictive, but if you have taken them for eight weeks or more, you may experience some 'discontinuation' effects if you stop taking them suddenly (see next question). These do not mean that the antidepressant is addictive as such. For a drug to be addictive or produce dependence, it must have a number of characteristics:

- it should produce a craving for the drug when the last dose 'wears off'

- it should produce tolerance, i.e. you need higher doses of the drug to achieve the same effect
- there should be an inability to reduce or control use
- it should produce withdrawal symptoms
- there should be continued use of the drug despite knowing of harmful consequences.

Thus, antidepressants, if stopped suddenly, may produce some 'discontinuation' symptoms, but these may be more of an 'adjustment' reaction from sudden removal of the drug rather than withdrawal.

Can I stop taking the tricyclics suddenly ?

It is unwise to stop taking tricyclics suddenly, even if you feel better. Two things could happen. Firstly, your depression can return if treatment is stopped too early (see '*For how long will I need to keep taking them?*'). Secondly, you might also experience some 'discontinuation' symptoms (see also above). At worst, these could include: headache, restlessness, diarrhoea, nausea, 'flu-like' symptoms, lethargy, abdominal cramps, sleep disturbance, and mild movement disorders. These symptoms can begin shortly after stopping or reducing doses, are usually short lived, will go if the antidepressant is started again, and can even occur with missed doses. If you get these discontinuation symptoms, you have a number of options:

- If they are not severe, you can wait for the symptoms to go—they usually only last for a few days or weeks
- Ask for something to help your symptoms in the short-term, e.g. a sedative or sleeping tablet
- Start the medication again (the symptoms should go) and then try reducing the dose more slowly over a longer time, e.g. reduce the dose by about a quarter (25%) every 4–6 weeks. Another system that works for some people is to use the syrup (if available); then, every time you take a dose, add some diluent (e.g. syrup or water) and then the syrup gradually (rather than suddenly) becomes more and more dilute.
- Switch to another antidepressant—this sometimes helps, e.g. fluoxetine has a long 'half-life' and is easier to stop than some antidepressants with shorter 'half-lives'.

When the time comes, your doctor should withdraw the drug slowly, e.g. by reducing the dose gradually every few weeks. You should discuss this with your doctor.

What should I do if I forget to take them?

Start again as soon as you remember, unless it is almost time for your next dose, then go on as before. Do not try to catch up by taking two or more doses at once, as you may experience more side-effects. You should tell your doctor about this at your next appointment.

If you have problems remembering your doses (as many people do) ask your pharmacist, doctor, or nurse about this. There are special packs, boxes, and devices available that can be used to help you remember.

Will the tricyclics make me drowsy?

These drugs may make you feel drowsy. You should not drive (see *Page 25*) or operate machinery until you know how they affect you. You should be careful as they may affect your reflexes or reaction times. However, they are not sleeping tablets and should not be treated as such, although if you take them at night they may help you to sleep.

Will the tricyclics cause weight gain?

Although a few people can lose weight on tricyclic antidepressants, some experience weight gain. This is partly due to increased appetite and/or a craving for carbohydrates or sweet food caused by the drugs. The tricyclics may also reduce your metabolic rate and you may not metabolise food as quickly, so not only do you eat more, you also use the food less efficiently. It is impossible to know what the effect on your weight may be because each person's experience is different. Unfortunately, all the tricyclic antidepressants seem to have the same effect.

If you do start to put on weight or have other weight problems, your doctor can arrange for you to see a dietician for advice. Usually, with expert advice about diet, any weight gained can be controlled while you are still taking this medication. However, in some people this weight gain is a serious problem. If it causes you distress make sure you tell your doctor. A change in drug, e.g. to a different type of antidepressants, or change in dose may be necessary and your doctor may want to arrange for you to see a dietician.

Will it affect my sex life?

Drugs can affect desire (libido), arousal (erection), and orgasmic ability. The tricyclics are known to affect all three stages in some people. Lack of desire and delayed orgasm is known to occur, although the opposite has been reported on rare occasions. If this does happen, discuss it with your doctor. A change in dose, timing, or drug may help to minimise problems. Any problem is not permanent.

Can I drink alcohol while I am taking these drugs?

You should avoid alcohol while taking these drugs as they can make you feel sleepier. This is particularly important if you need to drive or operate machinery, and you must seek advice on this.

Are there any foods or drinks that I should avoid?

You should have no problems with any food or drink other than alcohol (see above).

Will they affect my other medication?

You should not have any problems if you take other medications, although a few problems can occur. The tricyclic antidepressants can interact with 'MAOIs', some 'SSRIs' (especially fluoxetine ['Prozac®'] and paroxetine ['Seroxat®'] and some treatments for epilepsy. This does not necessarily mean they cannot be used together, just that you may need to follow your doctor's instructions very carefully. Make sure your doctor knows about all the medicines you are taking. Some other medicines, e.g. the painkiller, co-proxamol ('Distalgesic®') can make you drowsy. When combined with your tricyclic antidepressant, this could make you even drowsier. You should tell your doctor before starting or stopping these, or any other drugs. Recently, there has been much concern about the safety of St. John's wort with the tricyclics. Until more information is available, you should avoid taking St. John's wort when taking tricyclics.

What sort of side-effects might occur?

Side-effect	What happens	What to do about it
Common		
Drowsiness	Feeling sleepy or sluggish. It can last for a few hours after taking your dose	Do not drive or use machinery. Ask your doctor if you can take your tricyclic at a different time
Constipation	Feeling blocked up. You cannot pass a motion	Make sure you eat sufficient fibre, bran, or fruit, and drink enough fluid. Keep active and take plenty of exercise, such as walking. If this does not help, ask your doctor or pharmacist for a mild laxative
Dry mouth	Not much saliva or spit	Suck sugar-free boiled sweets. If it is severe, your doctor may be able to give you a mouth spray
Blurred vision	Things look fuzzy and you cannot focus properly	Do not drive with blurred vision. This should wear off after a few weeks. If it does not, see your doctor if you are worried. You will not need glasses
Weight gain	Increased appetite and putting on weight	A diet high in vegetables and fibre may help prevent weight gain. See also a separate question in this section
Sweating	Feeling hot and sticky. Your clothes may feel wet. This can happen particularly at night.	Tell your doctor at your next appointment. It is not dangerous but he/she may be able to adjust your dose.
Uncommon		
Nausea	Feeling sick	If it is severe, contact your doctor
Headache	Your head is pounding and painful	Try aspirin or paracetamol. Your pharmacist will be able to advise if these are safe to take with any other drugs you may be taking
Urinary retention	Not much urine passed	Contact your doctor now
Postural hypotension	A low blood pressure—this can make you feel dizzy when you stand up	Try not to stand up too quickly. If you feel dizzy, do not drive. This dizziness is not dangerous
Palpitations	A fast heart beat	It is not usually dangerous, and can easily be treated if it lasts a long time. Tell your doctor about it
Sexual dysfunction	Finding it hard to have an orgasm. No desire for sex	Discuss with your doctor. See also a separate question in this section
Rare		
Tremor	Feeling shaky	Contact your doctor now
Skin rashes*	Blotches seen anywhere*	Stop taking the drug and contact your doctor now*

Table adapted from UK Psychiatric Pharmacy Group leaflets, with kind permission (www.ukppg.org.uk)

Do not worry about this list of side-effects, as you may not experience any. There are other rare side-effects. If you develop any unusual symptoms ask your doctor about these at your next appointment.

If I am taking a contraceptive pill, will this be affected?

It is not thought that the contraceptive pill is affected by any of these drugs.

What if I want to start a family or discover I'm pregnant?

It is important to consider that there will be a risk to you and your child from taking a medicine during pregnancy, but also a possible risk from stopping the medicine, e.g., suffering a relapse. Unfortunately, no decision is risk-free. It will be for you to decide which is the least risk. All we can do here is to help you understand some of the issues, so that you can make an informed decision. For your information, major malformations occur 'spontaneously' in about 2–4% of all pregnancies, even if no drugs are taken. The main problem with medicines is termed 'teratogenicity', i.e. a medicine causing a malformation in the unborn child. A medicine causing teratogenicity is called a 'teratogen'. Since a baby has completed its main development between days 17 and 60 of the pregnancy (the so-called 'first trimester), these first 2–16 weeks are the main concern. After that, there may be other problems, e.g. some medicines may cause slower growth. The infant may also be affected after birth, e.g. withdrawal effects are possible with some drugs.

If possible, the best option is to plan in advance. If you think you could become pregnant, discuss this with your doctor and it may be possible to switch to medicines thought to carry least risk, and take other risk-reducing steps, e.g. adjusting doses, taking vitamin supplements, etc. If you have just discovered you are pregnant, don't panic, but, if possible, seek advice from your GP within the next few days. He or she may also want to refer you on to someone with more specialist knowledge of your medicine.

Very few medicines have been shown to be completely safe in pregnancy, so no manufacturer or advisor can ever say any medicine is safe. They will usually advise not to take a medicine during pregnancy, unless the benefit is much greater than the risk. In the UK, there is the NTIS (National Teratology Information Service), which offers individual risk assessments. However, its advice should always be used to help you and your doctor decide what is the risk to you and your baby. There is a risk from taking the medicine and a risk should you stop a medicine, e.g. you might become ill again and need to go back on the medication. The advice offered here is just that—advice, but may give you some idea about the possible risks and what (at the time of writing) is known through the medical press.

It may be helpful to know that in the USA, the FDA (Federal Drug Administration) classifies medicines in pregnancy in five groups:

A =	Studies show no risk, so harm to the unborn child appears only a remote possibility
B =	Animal and human studies indicate a lack of risk, but are not fully conclusive
C =	Animal studies indicate a risk, but there is no safety date in humans
D =	A definite risk exists, but the benefit may outweigh the risk in some people
X =	The risk outweighs any possible benefit

The tricyclics are classified as either 'C' or 'D'
- amitriptyline 'D'
- amoxapine 'C'
- clomipramine 'C'
- doxepin 'C'
- nortriptyline 'D'
- trimipramine 'C'.

The others are not available in the USA and so are not classified. One large study showed no evidence of a teratogenic effect and no increase in spontaneous abortions, although another study showed a very slightly increased rate of problems. Animal tests show a low risk of danger but some problems have been reported and so you should seek personal advice from your GP, who may then, if necessary, seek further specialist advice. There have been some reports of discontinuation effects (e.g. jitteriness) in the newborn child, and so it may be possible to reduce your dose a short time before your due date. One study has shown no evidence of any long-term effects on intelligence and language development.

Will I need a blood test?

Not usually. Some people who need to take higher doses occasionally need a blood test to make sure their dose of the drug is high enough, but not too high.

Can I drive while I am taking the tricyclic?

These drugs can affect your driving in two ways. Firstly, you may feel drowsy and/or suffer from blurred vision when beginning to take any of these drugs. Secondly, the drugs can slow down your reactions or reflexes. This is especially true if you also have a dry mouth, blurred vision, constipation (the so-called 'anticholinergic side-effects'). Until these wear off or you know how your drugs affects you, do not drive or operate machinery. You should take extra care, as they may affect your reaction times or reflexes even if you feel well.

It is an offence to drive, to attempt to drive, or to be in charge of a vehicle when unfit through drugs. It is advisable to let your insurance company know if you are taking these drugs. If you do not and you have an accident, it could affect your insurance cover.

If you are advised by your doctor not to drive, and continue to do so, the General Medical Council has advised doctors to inform the DVLA. The DVLA may then carry out an enquiry.

Drug group: 'Selective serotonin re-uptake inhibitors' (SSRIs or sometimes the '5-HT re-uptake blockers')

Drugs available	Brand name(s)	Forms available			
		Tablets	Capsules	Liquid	Injection
Citalopram	Cipramil®	✔		✔	
Escitalopram	Cipralex®	✔			
Fluoxetine	Prozac®		✔	✔	
Fluvoxamine	Faverin®	✔			
Paroxetine	Seroxat®	✔		✔	
Sertraline	Lustral®	✔			
Related drug*					
Trazodone *	Molipaxin®	✔	✔	✔(sugar-free)	

* This drug is included here for convenience (see below). Nefazodone (Dutonin) is related to trazodone, but was withdraw in 2003.

What are the SSRIs used for?

SSRIs are antidepressants that are used to help to improve mood in people who are feeling low or depressed. Fluoxetine ('Prozac®') may also be used to help treat the eating disorder 'bulimia nervosa'. Trazodone ('Molipaxin®') is not strictly an 'SSRI', but has many of the same effects, and so is included in this group for convenience. All these drugs are sometimes used to help other illnesses, e.g.

anxiety, bulimia nervosa, panic attacks, obsessive-compulsive disorder, and post traumatic stress disorder.

The SSRIs are now one of the most commonly prescribed antidepressants, but there are many other similar drugs. All these antidepressants seem to be equally effective at the proper dose, but have different side-effects to each other. Apart from nausea, the SSRIs generally have less side-effects than the older drugs. If one drug does not suit you, it may be possible to try another.

How do the SSRIs work?

The brain has many naturally occurring chemical messengers. One of these is called serotonin (or 5-HT) and is important in the areas of the brain that control mood and thinking. It is known that serotonin is not as effective or active as normal when someone is feeling depressed. The SSRI antidepressants increase the amount of the serotonin chemical messenger and this can help to correct the lack of action of serotonin and improve mood.

How should I take them?

Tablets and capsules:

Tablets and capsules should be swallowed with at least half a glass of water while sitting or standing. This is to ensure that they reach the stomach and do not stick in your throat.

Trazodone modified release tablets ('Molipaxin CR®') should be swallowed whole and not chewed. This is because they are made so that they release the drug over a longer period of time. This can help to reduce side-effects, or reduce the number of times a day you need to take your medicine. Crushing or chewing the tablets will cause the drug to be released too quickly.

Liquids:

Your pharmacist should give you a medicine spoon or oral syringe. Use it carefully to measure the correct amount. Ask your pharmacist for a medicine spoon if you do not have one.

When should I take the SSRI?

Take your medication as directed on the medicine label. Try to take it at regular times each day. If you are told to take your dose **once** a day this will usually be better in the morning, except with fluvoxamine, which is probably better in the evening. If you feel sick when first taking the SSRI, this should only last for a few days, but the nausea can be relieved by taking the medication with or after food. Also, taking the SSRI at mealtimes may be easier to remember, and there are no problems about taking any of these drugs with or after food. However, they are not sleeping tablets.

How long will the SSRI take to work?

It may take two weeks or more before the SSRIs start to have any effect on your mood, and a further three or four weeks for this effect to reach its maximum. If it has not started working in about six weeks, it is unlikely to work. Unfortunately, in some people, the effect may take a little longer to occur, e.g. several months if you are older.

For how long will I need to keep taking the SSRI?

This should be discussed with your doctor, as people's responses are different. To help you make a decision, it may be useful for you to know that research has shown that:

- for a first episode of major depression, your chances of becoming depressed again are much lower if you keep taking the antidepressant for six months after you have recovered (longer if you have risk factors for becoming depressed again)
- for a second episode, your chances of becoming depressed again are lower if you keep taking the antidepressant for one or two years after you have recovered
- for depression that keeps returning, continuing to take an antidepressant has been shown to have a protective effect for at least five years.

Are the SSRIs addictive?

SSRIs are not addictive, but if you have taken one of them (particularly paroxetine) for eight weeks or more, you may experience some 'discontinuation' effects if you stop taking it suddenly (see next question). These do not necessarily mean that the antidepressant is addictive as such. For a drug to be addictive, or to produce dependence, then it must have a number of characteristics:

- it should produce a craving for the drug when the last dose 'wears off'
- it should produce tolerance, i.e. you need a higher dose of the drug to achieve the same effect
- there should be an inability to reduce or control its use
- it should produce withdrawal symptoms
- there should be continued use of the drug despite knowing of harmful consequences.

All antidepressants, if stopped suddenly, may produce some 'discontinuation' symptoms, but these may be more of an 'adjustment' reaction from sudden removal of the drug rather than withdrawal.

Can I stop taking the SSRI suddenly?

It is unwise to stop taking them suddenly, even if you feel better. Two things could happen. Firstly, your depression can return if treatment is stopped too early (see '*For how long will I need to keep taking them?*'). Secondly, you might also experience some mild 'discontinuation' symptoms (see also above). At worst, these could include dizziness, vertigo/light-headedness, nausea, fatigue, headache, 'electric shocks in the head', insomnia, abdominal cramps, chills, increased dreaming, agitation and anxiety. They can start shortly after stopping or reducing doses, are usually short lived, will go if the antidepressant is started again and can even occur with missed doses. These effects have been reported for all the SSRIs, but it seems that they occur more often with paroxetine than any of the others. If you get these discontinuation symptoms, you have a number of options:

- If they are not severe, you can wait for the symptoms to go—they usually only last for a few days or weeks
- Ask for something to help your symptoms in the short-term, e.g. a sedative or sleeping tablet
- Start the medication again (the symptoms should go) and then try reducing the dose more slowly over a longer time, e.g. reduce the dose by about a

quarter (25%) every 4–6 weeks. Another system that works for some people is to use the syrup if available; every time you take a dose, add some diluent (e.g. syrup or water) and then the syrup gradually (rather than suddenly) gets more and more dilute

- Switch to another antidepressant—this sometimes helps, e.g. fluoxetine has a long 'half-life' and is easier to stop than is paroxetine.

When the time comes your doctor should withdraw the drug slowly, e.g. by reducing the dose gradually every few weeks. You should discuss this with your doctor.

What should I do if I forget to take a dose?

Start again as soon as you remember unless it is almost time for your next dose, then go on as before. Do not try to catch up by taking two or more doses at once, as you may experience more side-effects. You should tell your doctor about this at your next appointment.

If you have problems remembering your doses (as many people do) ask your pharmacist, doctor, or nurse about this. There are special packs, boxes, and devices available that can be used to help you remember.

Will the SSRI make me drowsy?

These drugs may make you feel drowsy, although this effect is less when compared to other antidepressants. You should not drive (see below) or operate machinery until you know how they affect you. You should take extra care, as they may affect your reaction times or reflexes. However, they are not sleeping tablets, although if you take them at night they may help you to sleep, especially trazodone.

Will the SSRI cause me to put on weight?

Fluoxetine ('Prozac®') may cause weight loss and usually the heavier you are the more you lose. Generally speaking, this 'side-effect' is not a cause for complaint. The other drugs in this group tend to have less effect on body weight. However, if you do start to have problems with your weight tell your doctor at your next appointment, who can then arrange for you to see a dietician for advice. It may be that in the long-term (i.e. over a year or more), there is a tendency to gain a little weight.

Will the drugs affect my sex life?

Drugs can affect desire (libido), arousal (erection), and orgasmic ability. The SSRIs are known to affect all three stages in some people. Delayed orgasm is known to occur in many people. Indeed some of these drugs are now widely used to help treat premature ejaculation. If this does seem to be happening, you should discuss it with your doctor, as a change in drug dose or the time when you take the dose may help to reduce problems.

A serious condition known as priapism has been reported with trazodone, but only rarely. Priapism occurs in men and is defined as a persistent, painful erection without sexual stimulation. It is not a cause for joking and should be treated as an emergency, as it can cause permanent damage. If these symptoms do happen, you should go to a hospital accident and emergency department as soon as possible, and certainly within two hours.

What sort of side-effects might occur ?

Side-effect	What happens	What to do about it
Common		
Nausea and vomiting	Feeling sick and being sick	Take your medicine after food. If you are sick for more than a day, contact your doctor. This tends to wear off after a few days. Starting at a lower dose for a few days may help
Insomnia	Not being able to fall asleep at night	Discuss with your doctor. He/she may change the time of your dose
Sexual dysfunction	Finding it hard to have an orgasm. No desire for sex	Discuss with your doctor. See also a separate question in this section
Less common		
Restlessness or anxiety	Tense and nervous, and you may sweat more	Try and relax by taking deep breaths. Wear loose-fitting clothes. This often happens early in treatment and should gradually ease off over several weeks. A lower starting dose may help, as may reducing the dose for a few days
Drowsiness	Feeling sleepy or sluggish. It can last for a few hours after taking your dose	Do not drive or use machinery. Ask your doctor if you can take your SSRI at a different time of day
Headache	Your head is pounding and painful	Try aspirin or paracetamol. Your pharmacist will be able to advise if these are safe to take with any other drugs you may be taking
Loss of appetite	Not feeling hungry. You may lose weight	If this is a problem, contact your doctor or pharmacist for advice
Diarrhoea	Going to the toilet more than usual and passing loose, watery stools	Drink plenty of water. Ask your pharmacist for advice. If it lasts for more than a day, contact your doctor
Rare		
Rashes and pruritis	Rashes anywhere on the skin. These may be itchy	Stop taking and contact your doctor now
Dry mouth	Not much saliva or spit	Suck sugar-free boiled sweets. If it is severe, your doctor may be able to give you a mouth spray
Skin rashes	Blotches seen anywhere	Stop taking and contact your doctor now. This is a particular problem with fluoxetine (Prozac®)
Tremors and dystonias	Feeling shaky. You may suffer from a twitch or feel stiff	It is not dangerous. If it troubles you, contact your doctor

Table adapted from UK Psychiatric Pharmacy Group leaflets, with kind permission (www.ukppg.org.uk)

Do not worry about this list of side-effects, as you may not experience any. There are other rare side-effects. If you develop any unusual symptoms, ask your doctor about these at your next appointment.

Much has been reported in newspapers and magazines about people who supposedly become more aggressive or suicidal when taking fluoxetine ('Prozac®'). Much has also been written implying that 'Prozac®' is a 'wonder drug'. It should be noted that:

- all antidepressants can cause a very few people to become more aggressive or suicidal. There is evidence suggesting that fluoxetine ('Prozac®') is the same as (or no worse than) other antidepressants in this respect
- there is no particular evidence that fluoxetine or any other drug in this group is a wonder drug, but they generally have less side-effects than the older antidepressants and are much less toxic.

Can I drink alcohol while I am taking the SSRI?

You should avoid alcohol except in moderation while taking these drugs as they may make you feel sleepier. This is particularly important if you need to drive or operate machinery, and you must seek advice on this. This is particularly the case with fluvoxamine ('Faverin®').

Are there any foods or drinks that I should avoid?

You should have no problems with any food or drink other than alcohol (see above).

Will the SSRI affect my other medication?

If you are taking 'Faverin®' (fluvoxamine) tablets, do not take indigestion remedies at the same time of day. This is because these tablets are 'enteric-coated'. Indigestion remedies contain alkalis, substances that can break down the coating of the tablet before it reaches the stomach. You may then experience more side-effects. If you need to take something for indigestion, wait for at least two hours after taking your 'Faverin®' tablets.

You should have no problems if you take other medications, although a few can occur. The SSRIs can 'interact' with 'MAOIs', lithium, tricyclic anti-depressants (e.g. amitriptyline, clomipramine, dothiepin), some anticonvulsants, antipsychotics (e.g. SSRIs) and anticoagulants, e.g. warfarin, although your doctor should know about these. This does not necessarily mean that the drugs cannot be used together, but you may need to follow your doctor's instructions very carefully. Make sure your doctor knows about all the medicines you are taking. Some other medicines, e.g. the painkiller, co-proxamol ('Distalgesic®'), or some of the antihistamines used for hay fever can make you drowsy. Recently, there has been much concern about the safety of St. John's wort with these drugs. Until more information is available, you should avoid taking St. John's wort when taking SSRIs. When combined with your SSRI, this could make you even drowsier. You should tell your doctor before starting or stopping these, or any other drugs.

If I am taking a contraceptive pill, will this be affected?

It is not thought that the contraceptive pill is affected by any of these drugs.

What if I want to start a family or discover I'm pregnant?

It is important to consider that there will be a risk to you and your child from taking a medicine during pregnancy, but also a possible risk from stopping the medicine, e.g. suffering a relapse. Unfortunately, no decision is risk-free. It will be for you to decide which is the least risk. All we can do here is to help you understand some of the issues, so that you can make an informed decision. For your information, major malformations occur 'spontaneously' in about 2–4% of all pregnancies, even if no drugs are taken. The main problem with medicines is termed 'teratogenicity', i.e. a medicine causing a malformation in the unborn child. A medicine causing teratogenicity is called a 'teratogen'. Since a baby has completed its main development between days 17 and 60 of the pregnancy (the so-called 'first trimester') these first 2–16 weeks are the main concern. After that, there may be other problems, e.g. some medicines may cause slower growth. The infant may also be affected after birth, e.g. withdrawal effects are possible with some drugs.

If possible, the best option is to plan in advance. If you think you could become pregnant, discuss this with your doctor and it may be possible to switch to medicines thought to carry least risk, and take other risk-reducing steps, e.g. adjusting doses, taking vitamin supplements, etc. If you have just discovered you are pregnant, don't panic, but, if possible, seek advice from your GP within the next few days. He or she may also want to refer you on to someone with more specialist knowledge of your medicine.

Very few medicines have been shown to be completely safe in pregnancy, so no manufacturer or advisor can ever say any medicine is safe. They will usually advise not to take a medicine during pregnancy, unless the benefit is much greater than the risk. In the UK, there is the NTIS (National Teratology Information Service) which offers individual risk assessments. However, their advice should always be used to help you and your doctor decide what is the risk to you and your baby. There is a risk from taking the medicine and a risk should you stop a medicine, e.g. you might become ill again and need to go back on the medication. The advice offered here is just that—advice, but may give you some idea about the possible risks and what (at the time of writing) is known through the medical press.

It may be helpful to know that in the USA, the FDA (Federal Drug Administration) classifies medicines in pregnancy in five groups:

A =	Studies show no risk, so harm to the unborn child appears only a remote possibility
B =	Animal and human studies indicate a lack of risk, but are not fully conclusive
C =	Animal studies indicate a risk, but there is no safety date in humans
D =	A definite risk exists, but the benefit may outweigh the risk in some people
X =	The risk outweighs any possible benefit

The SSRIs are classified as 'B' or 'C (fluoxetine, paroxetine and sertraline are 'B', citalopram and fluvoxamine are 'C'). The SSRIs are not teratogenic in animals, and most human data is for fluoxetine. No major abnormalities have been reported to date with paroxetine, but some 'discontinuation' effects (such as increased breathing rate and jitteriness) have been seen in a few infants for a couple of days after birth, so it may be wise to reduce the dose a little before your due date. Fluoxetine is the most widely studied SSRI in pregnancy. Information on over 2000 pregnancies indicates that the risk of 'spontaneous abortion' may be very slightly higher than normal, but that the number of abnormalities is the same as the general population and so fluoxetine does not appear to be a major risk. There is also no evidence of any long-term effect on intelligence and language development. There is little published data on the other SSRIs. You should, however, still seek personal advice from your GP, who may then, if necessary, seek further specialist advice.

Trazodone is classified as 'C'. There is no evidence of a teratogenic effect, and animal tests show a low risk of danger, but you should seek personal advice from your GP, who may then, if necessary, seek further specialist advice.

Will I need a blood test?

You will not need a blood test to check on your SSRI.

Can I drive while I am taking the SSRI?

You may feel drowsy at first when taking any of these drugs. Until this wears off, or you know how the drug affects you, do not drive or operate machinery. You should take extra care, as they may affect your reaction times.

It is an offence to drive, to attempt to drive, or to be in charge of a vehicle when unfit through drugs. It is advisable to let your insurance company know if you are taking these drugs. If you do not and you have an accident, it could affect your insurance cover.

If you are advised by your doctor not to drive, and continue to do so, the General Medical Council has advised doctors to inform the DVLA. The DVLA may then carry out an enquiry.

Drug: Mianserin

Drugs available	Brand name(s)	Forms available			
		Tablets	Capsules	Liquid	Injection
Mianserin	Bolvidon®	✔			

What is mianserin used for?

Mianserin is used to improve mood in people who are feeling low or depressed. There are many other antidepressants. All seem to be equally effective at the proper dose, but have different side-effects. If one drug does not suit you, it may be possible to try another.

How does mianserin work?

The brain has many naturally occurring chemical messengers. Two of these are called serotonin (or 5-HT) and noradrenaline. They are both important in the areas of the brain that control mood and thinking. It is known that these chemicals are not as effective or as active as normal when someone is depressed. Mianserin increases the amount of these chemical messengers released and this can help to correct their lack of action, thus improving mood.

How should I take mianserin?

Mianserin tablets should be swallowed with at least half a glass of water while sitting or standing. This is to ensure that they reach the stomach and do not stick in the throat. They should be swallowed whole and not chewed, as they have a special coating that helps to reduce side-effects. Crushing or chewing will cause the drug to be released too soon and you may experience side-effects, such as a numb mouth.

When should I take my mianserin?

Take your mianserin as directed on the medicine label. Try to take the drug at regular times each day. Taking it at mealtimes may make it easier to remember. There are no problems about taking this drug with or after food. If the instructions say to take it **once** a day, this is usually best taken at bedtime, as it may make you drowsy when first starting treatment. Mianserin is not, however, a sleeping tablet.

How long will mianserin take to work?

It may take two weeks or more before mianserin starts to have any effect on your mood, and a further three or four weeks for this effect to reach its maximum. If it has not started working in about six weeks, it is unlikely to work. Unfortunately, in some people, the effect may take a little longer to occur, e.g. several months if you are older.

For how long will I need to keep taking mianserin?

This should be discussed with your doctor, as people's responses are different. To help you make a decision, it may be useful for you to know that research has shown that:

- for a first episode of major depression, your chances of becoming depressed again are much lower if you keep taking the antidepressant for six months after you have recovered (longer if you have risk factors for becoming depressed again)
- for a second episode, your chances of becoming depressed again are lower if you keep taking the antidepressant for one or two years after you have recovered
- for depression that keeps returning, continuing to take an antidepressant has been shown to have a protective effect for at least five years.

Can I stop taking mianserin suddenly?

It is unwise to stop taking it suddenly, even if you feel better. Your depression can return if treatment is stopped too early. You may also experience some mild withdrawal symptoms (as explained above). When the time comes, your doctor will usually withdraw the drug slowly, e.g. by reducing the dose every few weeks. You should discuss this with your doctor.

What should I do if I forget to take a dose?

Start again as soon as you remember, unless it is almost time for your next dose, then go on as before. Do not try to catch up by taking two or more doses at once as you may experience more side-effects. You should tell your doctor about this at your next appointment. If you have problems remembering your doses (as many people do) ask your pharmacist, doctor, or nurse about this. There are special packs, boxes, and devices available that can be used to help you remember.

Will mianserin make me drowsy?

Mianserin may well make you feel drowsy. You should not drive (see below) or operate machinery until you know how it affects you. You should take extra care, as your reaction times may be affected. It is not, however, a sleeping tablet, although if you take mianserin at night it may help you to sleep.

Will mianserin cause weight gain?

It is not thought that mianserin causes changes in weight. If you do start to have problems with your weight, tell your doctor at your next appointment, as he/she can arrange for you to see a dietician for advice.

Will mianserin affect my sex life?

Drugs can affect desire (libido), arousal (erection), and orgasmic ability. It is not thought that mianserin has a significant effect on any of these.

Is mianserin addictive?

Mianserin is not really addictive, but if you have taken it for eight weeks or more, you may experience mild 'withdrawal' effects if you stop taking it suddenly. At worst these may include: sickness, anorexia, headache, giddiness, 'chills', and sleeplessness. These are very rare with mianserin.

What sort of side-effects might occur?

Side-effect	What happens	What to do about it
Common		
Drowsiness	Feeling sleepy or sluggish. It can last for a few hours after taking your dose	Do not drive or use machinery. Ask your doctor if you can take your mianserin at a different time
Constipation	Feeling 'blocked up' inside. You cannot pass a motion	Make sure you eat enough fibre, bran, or fruit and that you are drinking enough fluid. Keep active and take exercise, e.g. walking. If this does not help, ask your doctor or pharmacist for a mild laxative
Dry mouth	Not much saliva or spit	Suck sugar-free, boiled sweets. If it is severe, your doctor may be able to give you a mouth spray
Blurred vision	Things look fuzzy and you cannot focus properly	Do not drive. See your doctor if you are worried. You will not need glasses
Uncommon		
Postural hypotension	A low blood pressure—this can make you feel dizzy when you stand up	Try not to stand up too quickly. If you feel dizzy, do not drive. This dizziness is not dangerous
Very rare		
Agranulocytosis	Low numbers of white cells in the blood. You may catch more infections	Always tell your doctor or carer if you feel ill in any way. You may need a blood test. See also a separate question in this section

Table adapted from UK Psychiatric Pharmacy Group leaflets, with kind permission (www.ukppg.org.uk)

Do not worry about this list of side-effects, as you may not experience any. There are other rare side-effects. If you develop any unusual symptoms, ask your doctor about these at your next appointment.

Can I drink alcohol while I am taking mianserin?

You should avoid alcohol except in true moderation while taking mianserin, as it may make you feel sleepier. This is very important if you need to drive or operate machinery. You must seek advice on this.

Are there any foods, or drinks that I should avoid?

You should have no problems with any food or drink other than alcohol (see above).

Will mianserin affect my other medication?

You should have no problems if you take other medications, although a few problems can occur. Mianserin can 'interact' with some treatments for epilepsy, anxiety, and some sleeping tablets, although your doctor should know about these. This does not necessarily mean the drugs cannot be used together, just that you may need to follow your doctor's instructions very carefully. Make sure your doctor knows about all the medicines you are taking. Some other medicines, e.g. the painkiller co-proxamol ('Distalgesic®'), and some antihistamines (e.g. for hay fever) can make you drowsy. When combined with mianserin, this could make you even drowsier. You should tell your doctor before starting or stopping these, or any other drugs.

If I am taking a contraceptive pill, will this be affected?

It is not thought that the pill is affected by mianserin.

What if I want to start a family or discover I'm pregnant?

It is important to consider that there will be a risk to you and your child from taking a medicine during pregnancy, but also a possible risk from stopping the medicine, e.g. suffering a relapse. Unfortunately, no decision is risk-free. It will be for you to decide which is the least risk. All we can do here is to help you understand some of the issues, so that you can make an informed decision. For your information, major malformations occur 'spontaneously' in about 2–4% of all pregnancies, even if no drugs are taken. The main problem with medicines is termed 'teratogenicity', i.e. a medicine causing a malformation in the unborn child. A medicine causing teratogenicity is called a 'teratogen'. Since a baby has completed its main development between days 17 and 60 of the pregnancy (the so-called 'first trimester'), these first 2–16 weeks are the main concern. After that, there may be other problems, e.g. some medicines may cause slower growth. The infant may also be affected after birth, e.g. withdrawal effects are possible with some drugs.

If possible, the best option is to plan in advance. If you think you could become pregnant, discuss this with your doctor and it may be possible to switch to medicines thought to carry least risk, and take other risk-reducing steps, e.g. adjusting doses, taking vitamin supplements, etc. If you have just discovered you are pregnant, don't panic, but, if possible, seek advice from your GP within the next few days. He or she may also want to refer you on to someone with more specialist knowledge of your medicine.

Very few medicines have been shown to be completely safe in pregnancy, so no manufacturer or advisor can ever say any medicine is safe. They will usually advise not to take a medicine during pregnancy, unless the benefit is much greater than the risk. In the UK, there is the NTIS (National Teratology Information Service) which offers individual risk assessments. However, their advice should always be used to help you and your doctor decide what is the risk to you and your baby. There is a risk from taking the medicine and a risk should you stop a medicine, e.g. you might become ill again and need to go back on the medication. The advice offered here is just that—advice, but may give you some idea about the possible risks and what (at the time of writing) is known through the medical press.

It may be helpful to know that in the USA, the FDA (Federal Drug Administration) classifies medicines in pregnancy in five groups:

A =	Studies show no risk, so harm to the unborn child appears only a remote possibility
B =	Animal and human studies indicate a lack of risk, but are not fully conclusive
C =	Animal studies indicate a risk, but there is no safety date in humans
D =	A definite risk exists, but the benefit may outweigh the risk in some people
X =	The risk outweighs any possible benefit

Mianserin is not classified, as it is not available in the USA. There is no evidence of a teratogenic effect, but you should still seek personal advice from your GP, who may then, if necessary, seek further specialist advice.

Will I need a blood test?

You may need a blood test every four weeks when you start your mianserin tablets to ensure that they are not upsetting your blood system. This is usually only needed during the first three months of treatment.

Can I drive while I am taking mianserin?

You may feel drowsy and/or suffer from blurred vision when first taking mianserin. Until these symptoms wear off, or you know how your drug affects you, do not drive or operate machinery. You should take extra care, as it may affect your reaction times or reflexes.

It is an offence to drive, to attempt to drive, or to be in charge of a vehicle when unfit through drugs. It is advisable to let your insurance company know if you are taking mianserin. If you do not and you have an accident, it could affect your insurance cover.

If you are advised by your doctor not to drive, and continue to do so, the General Medical Council has advised doctors to inform the DVLA. The DVLA may then carry out an enquiry.

Drug: Mirtazapine

Drugs available	Brand name(s)	Forms available			
		Tablets	Capsules	Liquid	Injection
Mirtazapine	Zispin®	✔#		✔*#	

*Mirtazapine liquid is a special produced by Rosemont Pharmaceuticals
Zispin Soltabs (melt-on-the-tongue) are the standard preparation. The ordinary tablets were discontinued in March 2004

For what is mirtazapine used?

Mirtazapine is used to improve mood in people who are feeling low or depressed. There are many other antidepressants. All seem to be equally effective at the proper dose, but have different side-effects. If one drug does not suit you, it may be possible to try another.

How does mirtazapine work?

The brain has many naturally occurring chemical messengers (or 'neurotransmitters'). Two of these are called serotonin (or 5-HT) and noradrenaline. Both are important in areas of the brain that control mood and thinking. It is known that these chemical messengers are not as effective or as active as normal when someone is feeling depressed. Mirtazapine increases the amount of these chemical messengers and this can help to correct their lack of action, thus improving mood.

How should I take mirtazapine?

Mirtazapine tablets should be swallowed with at least half a glass of water while sitting or standing. This is to ensure that they reach the stomach and do not stick in the throat. They should be swallowed whole and not chewed.

When should I take my mirtazapine?

Take your medication as directed on the medicine label, usually once a day at bedtime. Try to take it at a regular time each day. If you need to take more than one dose a day, it may be easier to remember to take at mealtimes. There are no problems about taking this drug with or after food. However, you may prefer to take it at bedtime and it may help you to sleep, although mirtazapine is not a sleeping tablet.

How long will mirtazapine take to work?

It may take two weeks or more before mirtazapine starts to have any effect on your mood, and a further three or four weeks for this effect to reach its maximum, although recent studies suggest that mirtazapine may work slightly quicker than other antidepressants. If it has not started working in about six weeks, it is unlikely to work. Unfortunately, in some people, the effect may take a little longer to occur, e.g. several months if you are older.

For how long will I need to keep taking mirtazapine?

This should be discussed with your doctor, as people's responses are different. To help you make a decision, it may be useful for you to know that research has shown that:

- for a first episode of major depression, your chances of becoming depressed again are much lower if you keep taking the antidepressant for six months after you have recovered (longer if you have risk factors for becoming depressed again)
- for a second episode, your chances of becoming depressed again are lower if you keep taking the antidepressant for one or two years after you have recovered
- for depression that keeps recurring, continuing to take an antidepressant has been shown to have a protective effect for at least five years.

Is mirtazapine addictive?

Mirtazapine is not really addictive, but if you take it for eight weeks or more, you may experience some mild 'withdrawal' effects if you stop taking it suddenly. At worst, these may include: sickness, anorexia, headache, giddiness, 'chills', and sleeplessness. These are very rare indeed with mirtazapine.

Can I stop taking mirtazapine suddenly?

It is unwise to stop taking mirtazapine suddenly, even if you feel better. Your depression can return if treatment is stopped too early. In theory, you might also experience mild withdrawal symptoms, such as fatigue, nausea, and dizziness. When the time comes, your doctor will usually suggest that you withdraw the drug slowly, e.g. by reducing the dose every few weeks. You should discuss this with your doctor.

What should I do if I forget to take a dose?

Start again as soon as you remember unless it is almost time for your next dose, then go on as before. Do not try to catch up by taking two or more doses at once as you may experience more side-effects. You should tell your doctor about this at your next appointment. If you have problems remembering your doses (as many people do) ask your pharmacist, doctor, or nurse about this. There are special packs, boxes, and devices available that can be used to help you remember.

Will mirtazapine make me drowsy?

This drug may make you feel drowsy, particularly for the first week. This should then wear off. You should not drive (see below) or operate machinery until you know how it affects you. You should take extra care, as your reflexes (reaction times) may be affected. It is not, however, a sleeping tablet, although if you take it at night it may help you to sleep, especially the 'Zispin SolTab®'.

Will mirtazapine cause weight gain?

A few people can gain weight on mirtazapine. It seems that most people do not put on weight, but a few can gain quite a lot. If you have problems with your weight, your doctor can arrange for you to see a dietician for advice or consider switching to another drug.

Will it affect my sex life?

Drugs can affect desire (libido), arousal (erection), and orgasmic ability. Mirtazapine is not thought to have a significant effect on any of these.

Can I drink alcohol while I am taking mirtazapine?

You should avoid alcohol except in true moderation while taking mirtazapine, as it may make you feel sleepier. This is very important if you need to drive or operate machinery. You must seek advice on this. After a while, you may be able to try some alcohol and see how it affects you, but still be aware that it may affect your reaction times.

Are there any foods or drinks that I should avoid?

You should have no problems with any food or drink other than alcohol (see above).

Will mirtazapine affect my other medication?

You should have no problems if you take other medications. The only problem seems to be with some treatments to help you sleep, e.g. benzodiazepines. These can make you feel sleepier.

If I am taking a contraceptive pill, will this be affected?

It is not thought that 'the pill' is affected by mirtazapine.

What if I want to start a family or discover I'm pregnant?

It is important to consider that there will be a risk to you and your child from taking a medicine during pregnancy, but also a possible risk from stopping the medicine, e.g., suffering a relapse. Unfortunately, no decision is risk-free. It will be for you to decide which is the least risk. All we can do here is to help you understand some of the issues, so that you can make an informed decision. For your information, major malformations occur 'spontaneously' in about 2–4% of all pregnancies, even if no drugs are taken. The main problem with medicines is termed 'teratogenicity', i.e. a medicine causing a malformation in the unborn child. A medicine causing teratogenicity is called a 'teratogen'. Since a baby has completed its main development between days 17 and 60 of the pregnancy (the so-called 'first trimester') these first 2–16 weeks are the main concern. After that, there may be other problems, e.g. some medicines may cause slower growth. The infant may also be affected after birth, e.g. withdrawal effects are possible with some drugs.

If possible, the best option is to plan in advance. If you think you could become pregnant, discuss this with your doctor and it may be possible to switch to medicines thought to carry least risk, and take other risk-reducing steps, e.g. adjusting doses, taking vitamin supplements, etc. If you have just discovered you are pregnant, don't panic, but, if possible, seek advice from your GP within the next few days. He or she may also want to refer you on to someone with more specialist knowledge of your medicine.

Very few medicines have been shown to be completely safe in pregnancy, so no manufacturer or advisor can ever say any medicine is safe. They will usually advise not to take a medicine during pregnancy, unless the benefit is much greater than the risk. In the UK, there is the NTIS (National Teratology Information Service) which offers individual risk assessments. However, their advice should always be used to help you and your doctor decide what is the risk to you and your baby. There is a risk from taking the medicine and a risk should you stop a medicine, e.g. you might become ill again and need to go back on the medication. The advice offered here is just that—advice, but may give you some idea about the possible risks and what (at the time of writing) is known through the medical press.

It may be helpful to know that in the USA, the FDA (Federal Drug Administration) classifies medicines in pregnancy in five groups:

A =	Studies show no risk, so harm to the unborn child appears only a remote possibility
B =	Animal and human studies indicate a lack of risk, but are not fully conclusive
C =	Animal studies indicate a risk, but there is no safety date in humans
D =	A definite risk exists, but the benefit may outweigh the risk in some people
X =	The risk outweighs any possible benefit

Mirtazapine is classified as 'C'. There is no evidence available at the moment and so you should seek personal advice from your GP, who may then if necessary seek further specialist advice.

What sort of side-effects might occur?

Side-effect	What happens	What to do about it
Common		
Drowsiness	Feeling sleepy or sluggish. It can last for a few hours after taking your dose	This usually wears off after a week or so. Do not drive or use machinery. Ask your doctor if you can take your mirtazapine at a different time of day
Weight gain	Increased appetite and putting on weight	A diet high in vegetables and fibre may help prevent weight gain. See also a separate question in this section. If you increase your weight substantially, you may need to switch to another antidepressant
Rare		
Rashes and pruritis	Rashes anywhere on the skin. These may be itchy	Stop taking and contact your doctor now
Very rare		
Agranulocytosis	Low numbers of white cells in the blood. You may catch more infections	Always tell your doctor or carer if you have any unexplained fever, chill, sore throat, or mouth sores. You may need a blood test. See also a separate question in this section

Table adapted from UK Psychiatric Pharmacy Group leaflets, with kind permission (www.ukppg.org.uk)

Do not worry about this list of side-effects, as you may not experience any. There are other rare side-effects. If you develop any unusual symptoms, ask your doctor about these at your next appointment.

Will I need a blood test?

You should not need a blood test, but your doctor may need to check your blood occasionally.

Can I drive while I am taking mirtazapine?

You may feel drowsy when first taking this drug. Until this effect wears off, or you know how the drug affects you, do not drive or operate machinery. You should be careful as it may affect your reaction times or reflexes.

It is an offence to drive, to attempt to drive, or to be in charge of a vehicle when unfit through drugs. It is advisable to inform your insurance company that you are taking this drug. If you do not and you have an accident, it could affect your insurance cover.

If you are advised by your doctor not to drive, and continue to do so, the General Medical Council has advised doctors to inform the DVLA. The DVLA may then carry out an enquiry.

Drug: Moclobemide: (a RIMA or 'reversible inhibitor of monoamine oxidase-A')

Drugs available	Brand name(s)	Forms available			
		Tablets	**Capsules**	**Liquid**	**Injection**
Moclobemide	Manerix®	✔			

For what is moclobemide used?

Moclobemide is used to help improve mood in people who are feeling low or depressed. Moclobemide may also be used to help the symptoms of anxiety and a number of other symptoms.

There are many other antidepressants. All these drugs seem to be equally effective at the proper dose, but have different side-effects. If one drug does not suit you, it may be possible to try another.

How does moclobemide work?

There are many chemical messengers (or 'neurotransmitters') called 'monoamines' that occur naturally in the body. Some of these 'monoamines', e.g. serotonin and noradrenaline, have an effect on mood. If the levels of these 'monoamines' in the body are high, you may feel 'high' and if they are low you may feel 'low'. Moclobemide stops their breakdown by inhibiting the enzyme MAO-A, thus increasing the amount of monoamines to normal. This helps to improve mood in people who are feeling low or depressed.

How should I take moclobemide?

Tablets should be swallowed with at least half a glass of water while sitting or standing, so that they reach the stomach and do not stick in the throat. They should always be taken after meals.

When should I take it?

Take your moclobemide as directed on the medicine label. They should always be taken after meals with a drink of water. Try to take them at regular times each day.

How long will moclobemide take to work?

Moclobemide could take two weeks or more before starting to have an effect on your mood. It may then take a further three or four weeks for this effect to reach its maximum. If it has not started working in about six weeks, it is unlikely to work. Unfortunately, in some people, the effect may take a little longer to occur, e.g. several months if you are older.

For how long will I need to keep taking moclobemide?

This should be discussed with your doctor, as people's responses are different. To help you make a decision, it may be useful for you to know that research has shown that:

- for a first episode of major depression, your chances of becoming depressed again are much lower if you keep taking the antidepressant for six months after you have recovered (longer if you have risk factors for becoming depressed again)
- for a second episode, your chances of becoming depressed again are lower if you keep taking the antidepressant for one or two years after you have recovered
- for depression that keeps returning, continuing to take an antidepressant has been shown to have a protective effect for at least five years.

Is moclobemide addictive?

Moclobemide is not thought to be addictive.

Can I stop taking moclobemide suddenly?

It is unwise to stop taking moclobemide suddenly, even if you feel better (see above). The depression can return if treatment is stopped too early. When the time comes, your doctor should withdraw the drug slowly, e.g. by reducing the dose every few weeks. You should discuss this with your doctor.

What should I do if I forget to take a dose?

Start again as soon as you remember, unless it is almost time for your next dose, then go on as before. Do not try to catch up by taking two or more doses at once, as you may experience more side-effects. You should tell your doctor about this at your next appointment. If you have problems remembering your doses (as many people do) ask your pharmacist, doctor, or nurse about this. There are special packs, boxes, and devices available that can be used to help you remember.

Will moclobemide make me drowsy?

Moclobemide is unlikely to make you feel drowsy or sleepy. You should not, however, drive (see below) or operate machinery until you know how it affects you. You should take extra care, as it may affect your reaction times or reflexes. Some people find moclobemide makes them feel more alert or awake. It should not be used as a sleeping tablet.

Will moclobemide cause weight gain?

Moclobemide can cause you to feel less hungry, although this is not common. Studies have shown that there is generally no effect on body weight. However, a few people may have small weight changes. If you do start to put on or lose weight, or have other problems with your weight, your doctor can arrange for you to see a dietician for advice. Any weight change can be controlled with expert advice about diet, while you are still taking this medication. If it causes you concern, make sure your doctor knows about it. A change in drug or dose may be needed in some cases.

Will moclobemide affect my sex life?

Drugs can affect desire (libido), arousal (erection), and orgasmic ability. It is not thought that moclobemide has any significant effect on these, although some improvements in arousal have been reported.

What sort of side-effects might occur?

Side-effect	What happens	What to do about it
Common		
Dry mouth	Not much saliva or spit	Suck sugar-free boiled sweets. If it is severe, your doctor can give you a mouth spray
Headache	Your head is pounding and painful	Try aspirin or paracetamol. Your pharmacist will be able to advise if these are safe to take with other drugs you may be taking. Do not take anything containing codeine. If your headache persists, see your doctor
Insomnia	Not being able to sleep or stay asleep	Take your last dose no later than midday. Discuss with your doctor
Nausea	Feeling sick	Take your tablets after food. This should disappear after a few days. If nausea is severe, contact your doctor
Dizziness	Feeling light-headed and faint	Do not stand up too quickly. Try and lie down when you feel dizzy. Do not drive
Uncommon		
Agitation	Feeling restless or on edge	Try and relax by taking deep breaths. Contact your doctor if it worries you
Rare		
Bowel disturbance	You can suffer from diarrhoea or constipation	See your doctor or pharmacist for advice
Palpitations	A rapid heartbeat	This is not usually dangerous and can easily be treated if it lasts a long time. Tell your doctor about it
Tiredness	Feeling sleepy in the day	Discuss with your doctor. You may need to take it at a different time

Table adapted from UK Psychiatric Pharmacy Group leaflets, with kind permission (www.ukppg.org.uk)

Do not worry about this list of side-effects, as you may not experience any. There are other rare side-effects. If you develop any unusual symptoms, ask your doctor about these at your next appointment.

Contact your doctor immediately if you experience any of the following effects:

- severe headache (especially at the back of the head)
- light-headedness or dizziness
- flushing of the face
- pounding of the heart
- numbness or tingling of the hands or feet
- pain or stiffness in the neck
- nausea and vomiting, especially after eating, taking other medicines, or if it is unexpected or severe.

These effects are very unlikely, but could be the signs of a reaction to moclobemide.

Can I drink alcohol while I am taking moclobemide?

There should be no problems with drinking alcohol in moderation while you are taking moclobemide. It would, however, be wise not to drink very large amounts of Chianti wine, home made beers and wines, real ales and red wines. These contain tyramine (see the question about foods *below*) and could cause a reaction.

Will moclobemide affect my other medication?

Moclobemide can interact with a number of other medicines, although this does not necessarily mean the drugs cannot be used together, just that you may need to follow your doctor's instructions very carefully. However, the following should be avoided:

- pethidine
- codeine (e.g. in cough mixtures and some pain killers, such as 'Veganin®' or co-codamol)
- selegiline ('Eldepryl®'), which needs special care and dietary restrictions
- drugs, such as ephedrine, phenylpropanolamine, and pseudoephedrine, often found in cough and cold mixtures, e.g. 'Benylin®', 'Lemsip®', 'Night Nurse®'
- if you are taking cimetidine ('Tagamet®') for your stomach you may need a lower dose of moclobemide.

Your doctor should know about these, but make sure he/she does know about any other medicines you are taking and also that you tell your doctor before starting or stopping any other drugs. You also should follow these simple rules:

1. Only buy medicines from a pharmacy
- do not buy from supermarket shelves, drug stores, or newsagents
- do not take medicines given to you by friends or relatives, however well meaning they may be
- do not take medicines you purchased before moclobemide was prescribed unless you have first asked your doctor or pharmacist.

2. Take care over any medicines for coughs, colds, flu, hay fever, asthma, and catarrh
- if in doubt, ask your pharmacist.

Are there any foods or drinks that I should avoid?

Moclobemide acts by stopping the enzyme that breaks down a group of chemicals called monoamines in the body. Tyramine is an 'amino-acid' and a monoamine, which is found in many foods. If a person taking moclobemide eats these foods, the moclobemide stops tyramine from being broken down. The tyramine levels in the body then build up and cause a reaction (see under side-effects for warning signs of such a reaction). No special dietary restrictions are necessary when taking moclobemide, but some people may be especially sensitive to tyramine. You are advised to avoid eating large quantities of foods containing tyramine, e.g. strong and mature cheeses, yeast extracts ('Oxo®', 'Marmite®', 'Bovril®', and other meat or yeast extracts), and fermented soya bean products (found in some Chinese foods).

If I am taking a contraceptive pill, will this be affected?

It is not thought that the contraceptive pill is affected by moclobemide.

What if I want to start a family or discover I'm pregnant?

It is important to consider that there will be a risk to you and your child from taking a medicine during pregnancy, but also a possible risk from stopping the medicine e.g., suffering a relapse. Unfortunately, no decision is risk-free. It will be for you to decide which is the least risk. All we can do here is to help you understand some of the issues, so that you can make an informed decision. For your information, major malformations occur 'spontaneously' in about 2–4% of all pregnancies, even if no drugs are taken. The main problem with medicines is termed 'teratogenicity', i.e. a medicine causing a malformation in the unborn child. A medicine causing teratogenicity is called a 'teratogen'. Since a baby has completed its main development between days 17 and 60 of the pregnancy (the so-called 'first trimester'), these first 2–16 weeks are the main concern. After that, there may be other problems, e.g. some medicines may cause slower growth. The infant may also be affected after birth, e.g. withdrawal effects are possible with some drugs.

If possible, the best option is to plan in advance. If you think you could become pregnant, discuss this with your doctor and it may be possible to switch to medicines thought to carry least risk, and take other risk-reducing steps, e.g. adjusting doses, taking vitamin supplements, etc. If you have just discovered you are pregnant, don't panic, but, if possible, seek advice from your GP within the next few days. He or she may also want to refer you on to someone with more specialist knowledge of your medicine.

Very few medicines have been shown to be completely safe in pregnancy, so no manufacturer or advisor can ever say any medicine is safe. They will usually advise not to take a medicine during pregnancy, unless the benefit is much greater than the risk. In the UK, there is the NTIS (National Teratology Information Service) which offers individual risk assessments. However, their advice should always be used to help you and your doctor decide what is the risk to you and your baby. There is a risk from taking the medicine and a risk should you stop a medicine, e.g. you might become ill again and need to go back on the medication. The advice offered here is just that—**advice**, but may give you some idea about the possible risks and what (at the time of writing) is known through the medical press.

It may be helpful to know that in the USA, the FDA (Federal Drug Administration) classifies medicines in pregnancy in five groups:

A =	Studies show no risk, so harm to the unborn child appears only a remote possibility
B =	Animal and human studies indicate a lack of risk, but are not fully conclusive
C =	Animal studies indicate a risk, but there is no safety date in humans
D =	A definite risk exists, but the benefit may outweigh the risk in some people
X =	The risk outweighs any possible benefit

Moclobemide is not classified, as it is not available in the USA. There is no evidence of a teratogenic effect but you should still seek personal advice from your GP, who may then if necessary seek further specialist advice.

Will I need blood tests?

You will not need to have a blood test to check on your moclobemide.

Can I drive while taking moclobemide?

You may feel drowsy and/or suffer from blurred vision when first taking moclobemide. Until this wears off or you know how the drug affects you, you should not drive or operate machinery. You should take extra care, as it may affect your reaction times or reflexes.

It is an offence to drive, to attempt to drive, or to be in charge of a vehicle when unfit through drugs. It is advisable to inform your insurance company if you are taking this drug. If you do not and you have an accident, it could affect your insurance cover.

If you are advised by your doctor not to drive, and continue to do so, the General Medical Council has advised doctors to inform the DVLA. The DVLA may then carry out an enquiry.

Drug group: MAOIs (known in full as 'mono-amine oxidase inhibitors')

Drugs available	Brand name(s)	Forms available			
		Tablets	**Capsules**	**Liquid**	**Injection**
Isocarboxazid	Marplan®	✔			
Phenelzine	Nardil®	✔			
Tranylcypromine	(was Parnate®)	✔			

Tranylcypromine was marketed as 'Parnate®', but this trade name was dropped in 2002, although the same tablets are still available from the same company, but now just called tranylcypromine.

For what are the MAOIs used?

'MAOIs' are used to help improve mood in people who are feeling low or depressed. The MAOIs may also be used to help the symptoms of anxiety and a number of other symptoms.

There are many other antidepressants. All these drugs seem to be equally effective at the proper dose, but have different side-effects. If one drug does not suit you, it may be possible to try another.

How do the MAOIs work?

There are many chemical messengers (or 'neurotransmitters') called 'monoamines' that occur naturally in the body. One effect that monoamines have is on mood. If the levels of monoamines in the body are high you may feel 'high', and if they are low you may feel 'low'. MAOIs stop the breakdown of these monoamines by the MAO enzyme in the brain. By stopping this breakdown, the MAOIs increase the amounts of monoamines to normal. This helps to improve mood in people who are feeling low or depressed.

How should I take them?

Tablets should be swallowed with at least half a glass of water while sitting or standing, so that they reach the stomach and do not stick in the throat.

When should I take them?

Take your MAOIs as directed on the medicine label. Try to take them at regular times each day. If the label says to take your MAOIs **once** a day, this is usually better in the morning, as they can make you feel more alert. However, they have the opposite effect on some people, making them feel sleepy, although they are not sleeping tablets.

How long will the MAOIs take to work?

It may take two weeks or more before the MAOIs start to have any effect on your mood, and a further three or four weeks for this effect to reach maximum. If they have not started working in about six weeks, they are unlikely to work. Unfortunately, in some people, the effect may take a little longer to occur, e.g. several months if you are older.

For how long will I need to keep taking the MAOIs?

This should be discussed with your doctor, as people's responses are different. To help you make a decision, it may be useful for you to know that research has shown that:

- for a first episode of major depression, your chances of becoming depressed again are much lower if you keep taking the antidepressant for six months after you have recovered (longer if you have risk factors for becoming depressed again)
- for a second episode, your chances of becoming depressed again are lower if you keep taking the antidepressant for one or two years after you have recovered
- for depression that keeps returning, continuing to take an antidepressant has been shown to have a protective effect for at least five years.

Are the MAOIs addictive?

MAOIs are not addictive, but if you have taken them for eight weeks or more, you may experience some mild 'discontinuation' effects, if you stop taking them suddenly. These do not mean that the antidepressant is addictive as such. For a drug to be addictive or produce dependence, then it must have a number of characteristics, e.g:

- it should produce a craving for the drug when the last dose 'wears off'
- it should produce tolerance, i.e. you need more of the drug to generate the same effect
- there should be an inability to reduce or control use
- it should produce withdrawal symptoms
- there should be continued use of the drug despite knowing of harmful consequences.

Thus, antidepressants, if stopped suddenly, may produce some 'discontinuation' symptoms, but these may be more of an 'adjustment' reaction from sudden removal of the drug rather than withdrawal.

Can I stop taking the MAOIs suddenly?

It is unwise to stop taking MAOIs suddenly, even if you feel better. Two things could happen. Firstly, your depression can return if treatment is stopped too early (see '*For how long will I need to keep taking them?*'). Secondly, you might experience mild 'discontinuation' symptoms (see above). At worst, these could include confusion and delirium. The symptoms can start shortly after stopping, or reducing doses, are usually short lived, will go if the antidepressant is started again, and can even occur with missed doses.

When the time comes, your doctor should withdraw the drug slowly, e.g. by reducing the dose gradually every few weeks. You should discuss this with your doctor.

What should I do if I forget to take a dose?

Start again as soon as you remember, unless it is almost time for your next dose, then go on as before. Do not try to catch up by taking two or more doses at once, as you may experience more side-effects. You should tell your doctor about this at your next appointment.

If you have problems remembering your doses (as many people do) ask your pharmacist, doctor, or nurse about this. There are special packs, boxes, and devices available that can be used to help you remember.

What sort of side-effects might occur?

Side-effect	What happens	What to do about it
Common		
Postural hypotension	Feeling dizzy or faint after standing up	Do not stand up too quickly. If you feel dizzy, do not drive
Drowsiness	Feeling sleepy or sluggish in the daytime	Do not drive or use machinery
Dry mouth	Not much saliva or spit	Suck sugar-free boiled sweets. If it is severe, your doctor can give you a mouth spray
Constipation	Feeling 'blocked up' inside. You cannot pass a motion	Make sure you eat enough fibre, bran, or fruit and that you are drinking enough fluid. Keep active and take some exercise, e.g. walking. If this does not help, ask your doctor or pharmacist for a mild laxative
Uncommon		
Urine retention	Not much urine passed	Contact your doctor now
Headache	Your head is pounding and painful	Try aspirin or paracetamol. Your pharmacist will be able to advise if these are safe to take with other drugs you may be taking. If it is sudden or unexpected, be aware that this could be dangerous (see the separate question about foods to avoid)
Rare		
Oedema	Swelling in the legs	It is not dangerous. See your doctor
Sweating	Feeling hot and sticky. Your clothes may be wet	Contact your doctor. You will need to have your blood pressure checked
Insomnia	Not being able to fall or stay asleep	This is more common with tranylcypromine. Take your last dose before 3pm
Blurred vision	Things look fuzzy	Do not drive. Mention it to your doctor at your next appointment
Skin rashes	Blotches seen anywhere	Stop taking—see your doctor now

Table adapted from UK Psychiatric Pharmacy Group leaflets, with kind permission (www.ukppg.org.uk)

Do not worry about this list of side-effects, as you may not experience any. There are other rare side-effects. If you develop any unusual symptoms, ask your doctor about these at your next appointment.

Important

Contact your doctor immediately if you have any of the following effects:

- headache (especially at the back of the head)
- light-headedness or dizziness
- flushing of the face
- pounding of the heart
- numbness or tingling of the hands or feet

- pain or stiffness in the neck
- nausea and vomiting, especially after eating, taking other medicines, or if it is unexpected or severe.

These effects may be warning signs of a reaction.

Will the MAOI make me drowsy?

These drugs may make you feel drowsy or sleepy. You should not drive (see below) or operate machinery until you know how they affect you. You should take extra care, as they may affect your reaction times or reflexes. Some people find that MAOIs make them feel more alert or awake. MAOIs are not sleeping tablets.

Will it affect my sex life?

Drugs can affect desire (libido), arousal (erection), and orgasmic ability. However, it is not thought that the MAOIs have an effect on any of these.

Will the MAOI cause weight gain?

Although some people can lose weight on MAOIs, others have reported a weight gain, particularly with isocarboxazid and phenelzine. This is usually due to an increase in appetite and/or a craving for sweet food. It is impossible to know what the effect on your weight might be because the effect on each person will be different. If you do start to put on weight, or other have problems, your doctor can arrange for you to see a dietician for advice. Any weight increase can be controlled while you are taking this medication, with expert advice about diet. In some people this weight gain can be a serious problem. If it causes you distress make sure you tell your doctor. A change in drug or dose may be needed.

Can I drink alcohol while I am taking the MAOI?

It is best to avoid alcohol if you are taking MAOIs. If you do wish to drink you should follow these guidelines:

- totally avoid Chianti, home made beers and wines, real ales, and red wines
- drink white wines and non-alcoholic beers and lagers, but make sure you do not drink more than one or two units a day (i.e. one or two glasses, or up to a pint of beer or lager)
- gin, vodka, and other clear spirits are the safest, but should only be taken in true moderation, i.e. one or two measures a day.

Are there any foods or drinks that I should avoid?

MAOIs act by stopping the enzyme that breaks down a group of chemicals in the body called monoamines. Tyramine is an 'amino-acid' and a monoamine, which is found in many foods. If a person taking an MAOI eats these foods, the MAOI stops tyramine from being broken down. The tyramine levels in the body then build up and cause a reaction (see under side-effects for warning signs of such a reaction). There are a few general rules listed below that you should follow to help you avoid this reaction occurring:

- avoid foods that are matured or might be 'going off'
- avoid the foods listed below
- generally, the more 'convenience' the food, the safer it is, e.g. packet soups are safe. Although many foods have only small amounts of tyramine, it is possible to have local 'concentrations' that may cause a reaction.

Foods that must be avoided:

Dairy products: Hard cheeses, soft cheeses, and cheese spreads (e.g. Philadelphia) must be avoided. Foods containing cheese (e.g. pizzas, pies) must also be avoided. Small amounts of cottage cheese and 'Dairylea' cheese are probably safe.

Game, meat, and fish: Pickled or salted dried herrings, and any hung or badly stored game, poultry, or other meat that might be 'going off' must be avoided.

Offal: Avoid chicken liver pâté, liver pâté, and any other liver that is not fresh. Fresh chicken liver, fresh beef liver, and fresh pâté should be safe.

Fruit and vegetables: Broad bean pods and banana skins must be avoided (but the beans and the banana are safe). Avocado pears have been reported to produce a reaction and should be avoided if possible.

Yeast or meat extracts: Oxo®', 'Marmite®', 'Bovril®', and other meat or yeast extracts must be avoided. An alternative is gravy made with 'Bisto®' (i.e. 'Original®', 'Powder®', 'Rich Gravy Granules®', 'Onion Gravy Granules®', and 'Gravy Granules for Chicken®'), which is safe. Gravy made from juices of the roast or fresh meat should also be safe.

Bread is safe. 'Twiglets®' are sprayed with 'Marmite®' and a 50g bag could be enough to cause an unpleasant reaction.

Drinks: See the *'Can I drink alcohol?'* section above.

Will the MAOI affect my other medication?

The MAOIs can 'interact' with a number of other medicines, including other treatments for depression, high blood pressure, epilepsy, and some treatments for asthma. Your doctor should know about these, but make sure he/she knows all the medicines you are taking, and also that you tell your doctor before starting or stopping any other drugs. This does not necessarily mean the drugs cannot be used together, but you may need to follow your doctor's instructions very carefully. Recently, there has been much concern about the safety of St. John's wort with these drugs. Until more information is available, you should avoid taking St. John's wort when taking MAOIs.

There are a number of medicines that can be bought 'over-the-counter' from a pharmacy, chemist, supermarket, newsagent, etc. Many are **very** dangerous to take if you are also taking an MAOI. For example, many cough and cold cures could be dangerous, e.g. 'Benylin®', 'Lemsip®', or 'Night Nurse®'.
You should follow the following simple rules:

1. Only buy medicines from a pharmacy.

- do not buy from supermarket shelves, drug stores, newsagents
- do not take medicines given to you by friends or relatives, however well meaning they may be
- do not take medicines that you purchased before the MAOI was prescribed unless you have asked your doctor or pharmacist if these are safe.

2. Carry your MAOI card

- show it to any doctor, dentist, or pharmacist who may treat you.

3. *Take special care over any medicines for coughs, colds, flu, hay fever, asthma, and catarrh*

- these could be particularly dangerous
- if in doubt, ask your pharmacist.

If I am taking a contraceptive pill, will this be affected?

It is not thought that the contraceptive pill is affected by the MAOIs.

What if I want to start a family or discover I'm pregnant?

It is important to consider that there will be a risk to you and your child from taking a medicine during pregnancy, but also a possible risk from stopping the medicine, e.g., suffering a relapse. Unfortunately, no decision is risk-free. It will be for you to decide which is the least risk. All we can do here is to help you understand some of the issues, so that you can make an informed decision. For your information, major malformations occur 'spontaneously' in about 2–4% of all pregnancies, even if no drugs are taken. The main problem with medicines is termed 'teratogenicity', i.e. a medicine causing a malformation in the unborn child. A medicine causing teratogenicity is called a 'teratogen'. Since a baby has completed its main development between days 17 and 60 of the pregnancy (the so-called 'first trimester'), these first 2–16 weeks are the main concern. After that, there may be other problems, e.g. some medicines may cause slower growth. The infant may also be affected after birth, e.g. withdrawal effects are possible with some drugs.

If possible, the best option is to plan in advance. If you think you could become pregnant, discuss this with your doctor and it may be possible to switch to medicines thought to carry least risk, and take other risk-reducing steps, e.g. adjusting doses, taking vitamin supplements, etc. If you have just discovered you are pregnant, don't panic, but, if possible, seek advice from your GP within the next few days. He or she may also want to refer you on to someone with more specialist knowledge of your medicine.

Very few medicines have been shown to be completely safe in pregnancy, so no manufacturer or advisor can ever say any medicine is safe. They will usually advise not to take a medicine during pregnancy, unless the benefit is much greater than the risk. In the UK, there is the NTIS (National Teratology Information Service) which offers individual risk assessments. However, their advice should always be used to help you and your doctor decide what is the risk to you and your baby. There is a risk from taking the medicine and a risk should you stop a medicine, e.g. you might become ill again and need to go back on the medication. The advice offered here is just that—**advice**, but may give you some idea about the possible risks and what (at the time of writing) is known through the medical press.

It may be helpful to know that in the USA, the FDA (Federal Drug Administration) classifies medicines in pregnancy in five groups:

A =	Studies show no risk, so harm to the unborn child appears only a remote possibility
B =	Animal and human studies indicate a lack of risk, but are not fully conclusive
C =	Animal studies indicate a risk, but there is no safety date in humans
D =	A definite risk exists, but the benefit may outweigh the risk in some people
X =	The risk outweighs any possible benefit

The MAOIs are all classified as 'C'. There is a little evidence of a teratogenic effect and some problems have been reported, including possibly slower growth and so you should seek personal advice from your GP, who may then, if necessary, seek further specialist advice.

Will I need blood tests?

You will not need to have a blood test to check on your MAOI.

Can I drive while taking an MAOI?

These drugs can affect your driving in two ways. You may feel drowsy and/or suffer from blurred vision when first taking any of these drugs. Secondly, the drugs can slow down your reactions or reflexes. This is especially true if you also have a dry mouth, blurred vision, or constipation (the so-called 'anticholinergic side-effects'). Until these reactions wear off, or you know how your drug affects you, do not drive or operate machinery. You should take extra care as MAOIs may affect your reaction times or reflexes even if you feel well.

It is an offence to drive, to attempt to drive, or to be in charge of a vehicle when unfit through drugs. It is advisable to inform your insurance company if you are taking these drugs. If you do not and you have an accident, it could affect your insurance cover.

If you are advised by your doctor not to drive, and continue to do so, the General Medical Council has advised doctors to inform the DVLA. The DVLA may then carry out an enquiry.

Drug: Reboxetine

Drug available	Brand name	Forms available			
		Tablets	Capsules	Liquid	Injection
Reboxetine	Edronax®	4			

What is reboxetine used for?

Reboxetine is used to improve mood in people who are feeling low or depressed. All antidepressants seem to be equally effective at the proper dose, but have different side-effects to each other. If one drug does not suit you, it may be possible to try another.

How does reboxetine work?

The brain has many naturally occurring chemical messengers. Two of these are called serotonin (sometimes called 5-HT) and noradrenaline. Both are important in the areas of the brain that control or regulate mood and thinking. It is known that these two chemical messengers are not as effective or active as normal when someone is depressed. Reboxetine increases the amount of noradrenaline in the brain. This can help to correct the lack of action of this messenger and improve mood.

How should I take it?

Tablets should be swallowed with at least half a glass of water while sitting or standing. This is to ensure that they reach the stomach and do not stick in the throat.

When should I take my reboxetine?

Take your reboxetine as directed on the medicine label. Try to take it at regular times each day. Taking it at mealtimes may make it easier to remember, as there is no problem about taking this drug with or after food. If the instructions say to take the medication **once** a day, this is usually better at bedtime, as it may make you drowsy at first. However, reboxetine is not a sleeping tablet.

How long will reboxetine take to work ?

It may take two weeks or more before reboxetine starts to have any effect on your mood, and a further three or four weeks for this effect to reach its maximum. If it has not started working in about six weeks, it is unlikely to work. Unfortunately, in some people, the effect may take a little longer to occur, e.g. several months if you are older.

For how long will I need to keep taking reboxetine?

This should be discussed with your doctor, as people's responses are different. To help you make a decision, it may be useful for you to know that research has shown that:

- for a first episode of major depression, your chances of becoming depressed again are much lower if you keep taking the antidepressant for six months after you have recovered (longer if you have risk factors for becoming depressed again)
- for a second episode, your chances of becoming depressed again are lower if you keep taking the antidepressant for one or two years after you have recovered
- for depression that keeps returning, continuing to take an antidepressant has been shown to have a protective effect for at least five years.

Is reboxetine addictive ?

Reboxetine is not addictive, but if you have taken it for eight weeks or more you may experience some mild 'discontinuation' effects if you stop taking it suddenly, although nothing has yet been reported in the literature. For a drug to be addictive or produce dependence, it must have a number of characteristics:

- it should a produce craving for the drug when the last dose 'wears off'
- it should produce tolerance, i.e. you need more of the drug to achieve the same effect
- there should be an inability to reduce or control use
- it should produce withdrawal symptoms
- there should be continued use of the drug despite knowing of harmful consequences

If stopped suddenly, some antidepressants may produce 'discontinuation' symptoms, but these may be more of an 'adjustment' reaction from sudden removal of the drug rather than withdrawal. These are very rare with reboxetine.

Can I stop taking reboxetine suddenly ?

It is unwise to stop taking reboxetine suddenly, even if you feel better. Two things could happen. Firstly, your depression can return if treatment is stopped too early (see '*For how long will I need to keep taking it*?'). Secondly, you might also experience some mild 'discontinuation' symptoms (see above). When the time comes, it is better to withdraw the drug slowly, e.g. by reducing the dose gradually every few weeks. You should discuss this with your doctor.

What should I do if I forget to take it ?

Start again as soon as you remember unless it is almost time for your next dose, then go on as before. Do not try to catch up by taking two or more doses at once, as you may experience more side-effects. You should tell your doctor about this at your next appointment.

If you have problems remembering to take your doses, as many people do, ask your pharmacist, doctor, or nurse about this. There are special packs, boxes, and devices that can be used to help you remember.

Will reboxetine make me drowsy ?

Reboxetine should not usually make you feel very drowsy. You should take extra care when driving (see below) or operating machinery until you know how it affects you. You should be aware that reboxetine may affect your reflexes or reaction times.

What sort of side-effects might occur ?

Side-effect	What happens	What to do about it
Common		
Dry mouth	Not much saliva or spit.	Suck sugar-free boiled sweets. If it is severe, your doctor may be able to give you a mouth spray
Constipation	Feeling blocked up inside. You cannot pass a motion.	Make sure you eat enough fibre, bran, or fruit, drink enough fluid and that you keep active and take sufficient exercise, e.g. walking. If this does not help, ask your doctor or pharmacist for a mild laxative
Drowsiness	Feeling sleepy or sluggish. It can last for a few hours after taking your dose.	Do not drive or use machinery. Ask your doctor if you can take your reboxetine at a different time
Dizziness	Feeling light-headed and faint	Do not stand up too quickly. Try and lie down when you start feeling dizzy. Do not drive
Sweating	Feeling hot and sticky. Your clothes may feel wet. This can be more common at night.	Let your doctor know at your next appointment. It is not dangerous, but he/she may be able to adjust your dose(s)
Insomnia	Not being able to fall asleep at night	Discuss this with your doctor. He/she may be able to change the time of your dose or doses
Uncommon		
Palpitations	A faster heart beat	It is not usually dangerous and can easily be treated if it lasts a long time. Tell your doctor about it
Postural hypotension	A low blood pressure—this can make you feel dizzy when you stand up.	Try not to stand up too quickly. If you feel dizzy, do not drive. This dizziness is not dangerous
Urinary retention	Not much urine passed	Contact your doctor now
Rare		
Sexual dysfunction	Finding an orgasm difficult to achieve. No desire for sex.	Discuss with your doctor. See also a separate question in this section

Table adapted from UK Psychiatric Pharmacy Group leaflets, with kind permission (www.ukppg.org.uk)

Do not be worried by this list of side-effects, as you may not experience any. There are other rare side-effects. If you develop any unusual symptoms ask your doctor about these at your next appointment.

Will reboxetine cause me to put on weight ?

Although a few people can lose weight on reboxetine, others gain weight. It is impossible to know what the effect on your weight may be because the effect on each person will be different. If you do start to put on weight, or have other problems, your doctor can arrange for you to see a dietician for advice. While you are taking this medication, any weight gained can be controlled with expert advice about diet. In some people this weight gain can be a serious problem. If it causes you distress, make sure your doctor knows about it. A change in drug, e.g. to a different type of antidepressants, or a change in dose may be necessary.

Will it affect my sex life?

Drugs can affect desire (libido), arousal (erection) and orgasmic ability. Reboxetine is not thought to affect these three stages in most people. Lack of desire and impotence has been reported rarely. If you do experience this side-effect, you should discuss it with your doctor, as a change in dose, timing, or drug may help minimise problems. Any problem is reversible.

Can I drink alcohol while I am taking reboxetine ?

It is not thought that alcohol will make the side-effects of reboxetine worse. However, it is advisable to take alcohol only in moderation while taking reboxetine.

Are there any foods or drinks that I should avoid ?

You should have no problems with any food or drink other than alcohol (see above).

Will they affect my other medication ?

You should not have problems if you take other medications, although a few problems can occur with some drugs. Reboxetine can 'interact' with MAOI antidepressants, some cardiac drugs (e.g. dipyridamole, disopyramide, diuretics, flecainide, lidocaine, propafenone, beta-blockers), some 'SSRIs' (e.g. fluvoxamine), methadone, and some antibiotics (e.g. erythromycin). This does not necessarily mean they can not be used together, just that you may need to follow your doctor's instructions very carefully. Make sure your doctor knows about all the medicines you are taking. You should tell your doctor before starting or stopping these, or any other drugs.

If I am taking a contraceptive pill, will this be affected?

It is not thought that the contraceptive pill is affected by reboxetine.

What if I want to start a family or discover I'm pregnant?

It is important to consider that there will be a risk to you and your child from taking a medicine during pregnancy, but also a possible risk from stopping the medicine, e.g., suffering a relapse. Unfortunately, no decision is risk-free. It will be for you to decide which is the least risk. All we can do here is to help you understand some of the issues, so that you can make an informed decision. For your information, major malformations occur 'spontaneously' in about 2–4% of all pregnancies, even if no drugs are taken. The main problem with medicines is termed 'teratogenicity', i.e. a medicine causing a malformation in the unborn child. A medicine causing teratogenicity is called a 'teratogen'. Since a baby has completed its main development between days 17 and 60 of the pregnancy (the so-called 'first trimester'), these first 2–16 weeks are the main concern. After that, there may be other problems, e.g. some medicines may cause slower growth. The infant may also be affected after birth, e.g. withdrawal effects are possible with some drugs.

If possible, the best option is to plan in advance. If you think you could become pregnant, discuss this with your doctor and it may be possible to switch to medicines thought to carry least risk, and take other risk-reducing steps, e.g. adjusting doses, taking vitamin supplements, etc. If you have just discovered you are pregnant, don't panic, but, if possible, seek advice from your GP within the next few days. He or she may also want to refer you on to someone with more specialist knowledge of your medicine.

Very few medicines have been shown to be completely safe in pregnancy, so no manufacturer or advisor can ever say any medicine is safe. They will usually advise not to take a medicine during pregnancy, unless the benefit is much greater than the risk. In the UK, there is the NTIS (National Teratology Information Service) which offers individual risk assessments. However, their advice should always be used to help you and your doctor decide what is the risk to you and your baby. There is a risk from taking the medicine and a risk should you stop a medicine, e.g. you might become ill again and need to go back on the medication. The advice offered here is just that—**advice**, but may give you some idea about the possible risks and what (at the time of writing) is known through the medical press.

It may be helpful to know that in the USA, the FDA (Federal Drug Administration) classifies medicines in pregnancy in five groups:

A =	Studies show no risk, so harm to the unborn child appears only a remote possibility
B =	Animal and human studies indicate a lack of risk, but are not fully conclusive
C =	Animal studies indicate a risk, but there is no safety date in humans
D =	A definite risk exists, but the benefit may outweigh the risk in some people
X =	The risk outweighs any possible benefit

Reboxetine is not classified, as it is not available in the USA. There is no evidence of a teratogenic effect and animal tests show a low risk of danger, but you should still seek personal advice from your GP, who may then, if necessary, seek further specialist advice.

Will I need a blood test ?

You should not need blood tests.

Can I drive while I am taking reboxetine ?

Reboxetine should not affect your ability to drive. However, until you know how your drug affects you, take extra care when driving or operating machinery.

It is an offence to drive, to attempt to drive, or to be in charge of a vehicle when unfit through drugs. It is advisable to let your insurance company know if you are taking this drug. If you do not and you have an accident, it could affect your insurance cover.

If you are advised by your doctor not to drive, and continue to do so, the General Medical Council has advised doctors to inform the DVLA. The DVLA may then carry out an enquiry.

Drug: Venlafaxine

Drugs available	Brand name(s)	Forms available			
		Tablets	Capsules	Liquid	Injection
Venlafaxine	Efexor® Efexor-XL®	✔	✔		

For what is venlafaxine used?

Venlafaxine is used to improve mood in people who are feeling low or depressed. It can also be used to help anxiety and some other symptoms. There are many other antidepressants. All these drugs seem to be equally effective at the proper dose, but have different side-effects. If one drug does not suit you, it may be possible to try another.

How does venlafaxine work?

The brain has many naturally occurring chemical messengers (or 'neurotrans-mitters'). Two of these are called serotonin (or 5-HT) and noradrenaline. Both are important in the areas of the brain that control mood and thinking. It is known that these chemical messengers are not as effective or active as normal when a person is feeling depressed. Venlafaxine increases the number of these chemical messengers. This can help correct their lack of action and help to improve mood.

How should I take my venlafaxine?

The tablets and capsules should be swallowed with at least half a glass of water while sitting or standing. This is to ensure that they reach the stomach and do not stick in the throat.

When should I take it?

Take your medication as directed on the medicine label, usually twice a day, at breakfast and bedtime. Try to take it at regular times each day. It may be easier to remember to take it at mealtimes, and there are no problems in taking this drug with or after food. If the instructions are to take the medication **once** a day, this is usually better at bedtime, as it may make you drowsy at first. However, venlafaxine is not a sleeping tablet.

How long will venlafaxine take to work?

It may take two weeks or more before venlafaxine starts to have any effect on your mood, and a further three or four weeks for this effect to reach its maximum, especially if you are older. If it has not started working in about six weeks at the proper dose, it is unlikely to work.

For how long will I need to keep taking venlafaxine?

This should be discussed with your doctor, as people's responses are different. To help you make a decision, it may be useful for you to know that research has shown that:

- for a first episode of major depression, your chances of becoming depressed again are much lower if you keep taking the antidepressant for six months after you have recovered (longer if you have risk factors for becoming depressed again)
- for a second episode, your chances of becoming depressed again are lower if you keep taking the antidepressant for one or two years after you have recovered

- for depression that keeps returning, continuing to take an antidepressant has been shown to have a protective effect for at least five years.

Is venlafaxine addictive?

Venlafaxine is not addictive, but if you have taken it for eight weeks or more, you may experience some 'discontinuation' effects if you stop taking the drug suddenly. These do not mean that the antidepressant is addictive as such. For a drug to be addictive or produce dependence, then it must have a number of characteristics:

- it should produce a craving for the drug when the last dose 'wears off'
- it should produce tolerance, i.e. you need more of the drug to achieve the same effect
- there should be an inability to reduce or control use
- it should produce withdrawal symptoms
- there should be continued use of the drug despite knowing of harmful consequences.

If stopped suddenly, all antidepressants may produce some 'discontinuation' symptoms, but these may be more of an 'adjustment' reaction from sudden removal of the drug rather than withdrawal (see also next question).

Can I stop taking venlafaxine suddenly?

It is unwise to stop taking venlafaxine suddenly, even if you feel better. Two things could happen. Firstly, your depression can return if treatment is stopped too early (see *'For how long will I need to keep taking them?'*). Secondly, you may experience 'discontinuation' symptoms (see above). At worst, these could include: dizziness, vertigo, light-headedness, nausea, fatigue, headache, 'electric shocks in the head', insomnia, abdominal cramps, chills, increased dreaming, agitation, and anxiety. They can start shortly after stopping or reducing doses, are usually short lived, will go if the antidepressant is started again, and can even occur with missed doses. If you get these discontinuation symptoms, you have a number of options:

- If they are not severe, you can wait for the symptoms to go—they usually only last for a few days or weeks
- Ask for something to help your symptoms in the short-term, e.g. a sedative or sleeping tablet
- Start the medication again (the symptoms should go) and then try reducing the dose more slowly over a longer time, e.g. reduce the dose by about a quarter (25%) every 4–6 weeks
- Switch to another antidepressant—this sometimes helps, e.g. fluoxetine has a long 'half-life' and may be easier to stop than venlafaxine, for example.

When the time comes, your doctor should withdraw the drug slowly, e.g. by reducing the dose gradually every few weeks. You should discuss this with your doctor.

What should I do if I forget to take a dose?

Start again as soon as you remember unless it is almost time for your next dose, then go on as before. Do not try to catch up by taking two or more doses at once, as you may experience more side-effects. You should tell your doctor about this at your next appointment. If you have problems remembering your doses (as many people do) ask your pharmacist, doctor, or nurse about this. There are special packs, boxes, and devices available that can be used to help you remember.

Will venlafaxine make me drowsy?

This drug may make you feel a little drowsy. You should not drive or operate machinery until you know how it affects you. You should take extra care, as it may affect your reflexes or reaction times. It is not, however, a sleeping tablet, although if you take it at night it may help you to sleep.

Will venlafaxine cause weight gain?

A few people can lose weight on venlafaxine, unlike some of the older antidepressants where weight gain is more common. If you have problems with your weight, your doctor can arrange for you to see a dietician for advice.

Will venlafaxine affect my sex life?

Drugs can affect desire (libido), arousal (erection), and orgasmic ability. Venlafaxine has been reported to affect all three stages in some people. Delayed orgasm is known to occur in many people. If this does seem to be happening, you should discuss it with your doctor, as a change in dose, timing, or drug may help reduce any problem.

What type of side-effects might occur?

Side-effect	What happens	What to do about it
Common		
Nausea	Feeling sick	If it is severe, contact your doctor. Taking the sustained release version (XL) may help to relieve it
Headache	Your head is pounding and painful	Try aspirin or paracetamol. Your pharmacist will be able to advise if these are safe to take with other drugs you may be taking
Drowsiness	Feeling sleepy or sluggish. This can last for a few hours	Do not drive or use machinery. Ask your doctor if you can take your venlafaxine at a different time
Dizziness	Feeling lightheaded and faint	Your dose may be too high, contact your doctor. Do not stand up too quickly. Try and lie down when you feel it coming on. Do not drive
Uncommon		
Sleep disturbances	You cannot sleep very well	If you feel like this for more than a week after starting venlafaxine, tell your doctor
Hypotension	Low blood pressure—this can make you feel dizzy	Try not to stand up too quickly. If you feel dizzy, do not drive. This dizziness is not dangerous, but you may need to have your blood pressure checked
Weight gain	Larger appetite and increase in weight	A diet high in vegetables and fibre may help prevent weight gain. See also a separate question in this section
Wheeziness	You find it difficult to breathe and your chest feels tight	Contact your doctor now
Sexual dysfunction	Finding it hard to have an orgasm. No desire for sex	Discuss with your doctor. See also a separate question in this section
Rare		
Skin rashes	Blotches seen anywhere	Stop taking and contact your doctor now

Table adapted from UK Psychiatric Pharmacy Group leaflets, with kind permission (www.ukppg.org.uk)

Do not worry about this list of side-effects, as you may not experience any. There are other rare side-effects. If you develop any unusual symptoms, ask your doctor about these at your next appointment.

Can I drink alcohol while I am taking venlafaxine?

You should avoid alcohol while taking venlafaxine, as it may make you feel sleepier. This is particularly important if you need to drive or operate machinery. You must seek advice on this.

Are there any foods or drinks that I should avoid?

You should have no problems with any food or drink other than alcohol (see above).

Will venlafaxine affect my other medication?

You should have no problems if you take other medications. The only problem seems to be with a treatment for indigestion or stomach ulcers called cimetidine ('Tagamet®'), which you can buy over-the-counter. This can make the side-effects of venlafaxine worse. Recently, there has been much concern about the safety of St. John's wort with many drugs. Until more information is available, you should avoid taking St. John's wort when taking venlafaxine.

If I am taking a contraceptive pill, will this be affected?

It is not thought that venlafaxine affects the contraceptive pill.

What if I want to start a family or discover I'm pregnant?

It is important to consider that there will be a risk to you and your child from taking a medicine during pregnancy, but also a possible risk from stopping the medicine e.g., suffering a relapse. Unfortunately, no decision is risk-free. It will be for you to decide which is the least risk. All we can do here is to help you understand some of the issues, so that you can make an informed decision. For your information, major malformations occur 'spontaneously' in about 2–4% of all pregnancies, even if no drugs are taken. The main problem with medicines is termed 'teratogenicity', i.e. a medicine causing a malformation in the unborn child. A medicine causing teratogenicity is called a 'teratogen'. Since a baby has completed its main development between days 17 and 60 of the pregnancy (the so-called 'first trimester'), these first 2–16 weeks are the main concern. After that, there may be other problems, e.g. some medicines may cause slower growth. The infant may also be affected after birth, e.g. withdrawal effects are possible with some drugs.

If possible, the best option is to plan in advance. If you think you could become pregnant, discuss this with your doctor and it may be possible to switch to medicines thought to carry least risk, and take other risk-reducing steps, e.g. adjusting doses, taking vitamin supplements, etc. If you have just discovered you are pregnant, don't panic, but, if possible, seek advice from your GP within the next few days. He or she may also want to refer you on to someone with more specialist knowledge of your medicine.

Very few medicines have been shown to be completely safe in pregnancy, so no manufacturer or advisor can ever say any medicine is safe. They will usually advise not to take a medicine during pregnancy, unless the benefit is much greater than the risk. In the UK, there is the NTIS (National Teratology Information Service) which offers individual risk assessments. However, their advice should always be used to help you and your doctor decide what is the risk to you and your baby. There is a risk from taking the medicine and a risk should you stop a medicine, e.g. you might become ill again and need to go back on the medication. The advice offered here is just that—**advice**, but may give you some idea about the possible risks and what (at the time of writing) is known through the medical press.

It may be helpful to know that in the USA, the FDA (Federal Drug Administration) classifies medicines in pregnancy in five groups:

A =	Studies show no risk, so harm to the unborn child appears only a remote possibility
B =	Animal and human studies indicate a lack of risk, but are not fully conclusive
C =	Animal studies indicate a risk, but there is no safety date in humans
D =	A definite risk exists, but the benefit may outweigh the risk in some people
X =	The risk outweighs any possible benefit

Venlafaxine is classified as 'C', and the manufacturers, Wyeth, recommend it should not be taken in pregnancy. There is no evidence available at the moment and so you should seek personal advice from your GP, who may then, if necessary, seek further specialist advice.

Will I need a blood test?

You should not need a blood test, but your doctor may need to check your blood occasionally.

Can I drive while I am taking venlafaxine?

You may feel drowsy or sleepy and suffer from blurred vision when first taking this drug. Until these effects wear off or you know how the drug affects you, do not drive or operate machinery. You should take extra care, as it may affect your reaction times or reflexes.

It is an offence to drive, to attempt to drive, or to be in charge of a vehicle when unfit through drugs. It is advisable to let your insurance company know if you are taking this drug. If you do not and you have an accident, it could affect your insurance cover.

If you are advised by your doctor not to drive, and continue to do so, the General Medical Council has advised doctors to inform the DVLA. The DVLA may then carry out an enquiry.

Drug group: Flupentixol (or flupenthixol)(low dose)

Drugs available	Brand name(s)	Forms available			
		Tablets	**Capsules**	**Liquid**	**Injection**
Flupentixol	Fluanxol®	✔			

For what is flupentixol used?

Flupentixol is used in low doses (e.g. up to 2 to 3mg a day) as an antidepressant to help improve mood in people who are feeling low or depressed. It may also be used to help the symptoms of anxiety. There are many other antidepressants. All these drugs seem to be equally effective at the proper dose, but have different side-effects. If one drug does not suit you, it may be possible to try another. At higher doses, flupentixol is used to help the symptoms of some other mental health problems (see under antipsychotics for these uses).

How does flupentixol work?

The brain has many naturally occurring chemical messengers (or 'neurotransmitters'). Two of these are called serotonin (or 5-HT) and noradrenaline. Both are important in the areas of the brain that control mood and thinking. It is known that these chemical messengers are not as effective or active as normal when a person is depressed. Flupentixol may increase the quantity of these chemical messengers released in the brain and this can help correct their lack of action and improve mood. It also has a calming action.

How should I take it?

The tablets should be swallowed with at least half a glass of water while sitting or standing. This is to ensure that they reach the stomach and do not stick in the throat.

When should I take it?

Take your medication as directed on the medicine label. Try to take it at regular times each day. It may be easier to remember to take at mealtimes, and there is no problem about taking flupentixol with or after food. If you are told to take it **once** a day, this should be in the morning as it may make you more alert. If you have to take it more than once each day, the last dose should be taken no later than 4pm to make sure that you are not kept awake when you go to bed.

How long will flupentixol take to work?

Your doctor will probably increase your dose of flupentixol tablets gradually over the first few weeks of treatment. If it has had no effect on your mood after four weeks, your doctor may want to try another treatment. You should discuss this with your doctor. If it has not started working in about six weeks, it is unlikely to work. Unfortunately, in some people, the effect may take a little longer to occur, e.g. several months if you are older.

For how long will I need to keep taking flupentixol?

This should be discussed with your doctor, as people's responses are different. Some people may need to continue taking the drug for months or even years. It is usually necessary to take it for at least a month after you have recovered. Usually it is better to take it for at least 6–12 months to make sure you are fully recovered from your illness. If you have been depressed more than once, it is better to keep taking an antidepressant for several years, as this will reduce the chance of you becoming ill again.

Is flupentixol addictive?

Flupentixol is not addictive.

Can I stop taking flupentixol suddenly?

Although you should not suffer any withdrawal effects, it is unwise to stop taking flupentixol suddenly, even if you feel better. Flupentixol tablets must be taken every day if they are to continue to work. If you do stop taking them before you are advised to do so by your doctor, your symptoms could return.

What should I do if I forget to take a dose?

Start again as soon as you remember unless it is almost time for your next dose, then go on as before. Do not try to catch up by taking two or more doses at once, as you may experience more side-effects. You should tell your doctor about this at your next appointment.

If you have problems remembering your doses (as many people do) ask your pharmacist, doctor, or nurse about this. There are special packs, boxes, and devices available that can be used to help you remember.

Will flupentixol make me drowsy?

This drug may make you feel drowsy. You should not drive (see below) or operate machinery until you know how it affects you. You should take extra care, as it may affect your reaction times.

Flupentixol can also have an alerting effect in some people so it should not be taken later than 4pm each afternoon.

Will flupentixol cause weight gain?

In low doses it is not thought that flupentixol causes any changes in weight. However, if you do start to put on weight, tell your doctor at your next appointment, as he/she can arrange for you to see a dietician for advice.

Will flupentixol affect my sex life?

Drugs can affect desire (libido), arousal (erection), and orgasmic ability. Flupentixol is not thought to significantly affect any of these.

What sort of side-effects might occur?

Side-effect	What happens	What to do about it
Common		
Drowsiness	Feeling sleepy or sluggish. This can last for a few hours, or longer after taking your dose	Do not drive or use machinery. Ask your doctor if you can take the flupentixol at a different time of day
Sleep disturbances	You cannot sleep very well	If you feel like this for more than a week after starting flupentixol, tell your doctor. It is advisable not to take a dose after 4pm in the afternoon, as this can make sleep problems worse
Uncommon		
Movement disorders (extra-pyramidal or Parkinsonian side-effects)	Having shaky hands and feeling shaky. Your neck may twist back. Your eyes and tongue may move on their own. You may feel very restless	It is not usually dangerous and is a well known side-effect, although uncommon at the dose used to help depression

Table adapted from UK Psychiatric Pharmacy Group leaflets, with kind permission (www.ukppg.org.uk)

Do not worry about this list of side-effects, as you may not experience any. There are many other rare side-effects including headache, dizziness, and tremor. If you experience any unusual symptoms, ask your doctor about these at your next appointment.

Can I drink alcohol while I am taking flupentixol?

You should avoid alcohol while taking this drug, as it may make you feel sleepy. This is particularly important if you need to drive or operate machinery, and you must seek advice on this.

Are there any foods or drinks that I should avoid?

You should have no problems with any food or drink other than alcohol (see above).

Will flupentixol affect my other medication?

You should have no problems if you take other medications, although a few problems can occur. Flupentixol can 'interact' with some other antidepressants and some anticonvulsants, although your doctor should know about these. This does not necessarily mean the drugs cannot be used together, just that you may need to follow your doctor's instructions very carefully. Make sure your doctor knows about all the medicines you are taking. Some other medicines, e.g. the painkiller co-proxamol, can make you drowsy. When combined with your flupentixol, this could make you even drowsier. You should tell your doctor before starting or stopping these, or any other drugs.

If I am taking a contraceptive pill, will this be affected?

It is not thought that the contraceptive pill is affected by flupentixol.

What if I want to start a family or discover I'm pregnant?

It is important to consider that there will be a risk to you and your child from taking a medicine during pregnancy, but also a possible risk from stopping the medicine, e.g., suffering a relapse. Unfortunately, no decision is risk-free. It will be for you to decide which is the least risk. All we can do here is to help you understand some of the issues, so that you can make an informed decision. For your information, major malformations occur 'spontaneously' in about 2–4% of all pregnancies, even if no drugs are taken. The main problem with medicines is termed 'teratogenicity', i.e. a medicine causing a malformation in the unborn child. A medicine causing teratogenicity is called a 'teratogen'. Since a baby has completed its main development between days 17 and 60 of the pregnancy (the so-called 'first trimester), these first 2–16 weeks are the main concern. After that, there may be other problems, e.g. some medicines may cause slower growth. The infant may also be affected after birth, e.g. withdrawal effects are possible with some drugs.

If possible, the best option is to plan in advance. If you think you could become pregnant, discuss this with your doctor and it may be possible to switch to medicines thought to carry least risk, and take other risk-reducing steps, e.g. adjusting doses, taking vitamin supplements, etc. If you have just discovered you are pregnant, don't panic, but, if possible, seek advice from your GP within the next few days. He or she may also want to refer you on to someone with more specialist knowledge of your medicine.

Very few medicines have been shown to be completely safe in pregnancy, so no manufacturer or advisor can ever say any medicine is safe. They will usually advise not to take a medicine during pregnancy, unless the benefit is much greater than the risk. In the UK, there is the NTIS (National Teratology Information Service) which offers individual risk assessments. However, their advice should always be used to help you and your doctor decide what is the risk to you and your baby. There is a risk from taking the medicine and a risk should you stop a medicine, e.g. you might become ill again and need to go back on the medication. The advice offered here is just that—**advice**, but may give you some idea about the possible risks and what (at the time of writing) is known through the medical press.

It may be helpful to know that in the USA, the FDA (Federal Drug Administration) classifies medicines in pregnancy in five groups:

A =	Studies show no risk, so harm to the unborn child appears only a remote possibility
B =	Animal and human studies indicate a lack of risk, but are not fully conclusive
C =	Animal studies indicate a risk, but there is no safety date in humans
D =	A definite risk exists, but the benefit may outweigh the risk in some people
X =	The risk outweighs any possible benefit

Flupentixol is not classified, as it is not available in the USA. There is no evidence of a teratogenic effect, animal tests show a low risk of danger, but some problems have been reported and so you should seek personal advice from your GP, who may then, if necessary, seek further specialist advice.

Will I need a blood test?

You should not need to have a blood test.

Can I drive while I am taking flupentixol?

Flupentixol can affect your driving in two ways. You may feel drowsy and/or suffer from blurred vision when first taking this drug. Secondly, it can slow down your reactions or reflexes. This is especially true if you also have a dry mouth, blurred vision, constipation, etc (the so-called 'anticholinergic side-effects'). Until these wear off or you know how your drug affects you, do not drive or operate machinery. You should take extra care, as it may affect your reaction times or reflexes even though you feel well.

It is advisable to let your insurance company know if you are taking this drug. If you do not and you have an accident, it could affect your insurance cover.

If you are advised by your doctor not to drive, and continue to do so, the General Medical Council has advised doctors to inform the DVLA. The DVLA may then carry out an enquiry.

Drug: Tryptophan or L-Tryptophan

Drugs available	Brand name(s)	Forms available			
		Tablets	**Capsules**	**Liquid**	**Injection**
Tryptophan	Optimax®	✔			

For what is tryptophan used?

Tryptophan is a naturally occurring substance that helps to improve mood in people who are feeling low or depressed. It is, in fact, an 'amino-acid' and is found in many foods. It is usually used with other antidepressants, as tryptophan seems to work better with other drugs than it does on its own.

How does tryptophan work?

The brain has many naturally occurring chemical messengers ('neurotransmitters'). One of these is called serotonin, or 5-HT. It is known that a low level of serotonin (5-HT) occurs in the brains of people who are feeling depressed. Tryptophan is converted into serotonin in the body. If you take tryptophan tablets, this can increase the amount of serotonin in the brain and help to improve your mood.

How should I take it?

The tablets should be swallowed with at least half a glass of water while sitting or standing. This is to ensure that they reach the stomach and do not stick in your throat.

When should I take it?

Take your medication as directed on the medicine label. Try to take your doses at regular times each day. You may feel a little sick when you first start taking tryptophan. This should only last for two or three days, but taking your tryptophan after food can help. Taking it after meals may also make it easier for you to remember to take your medicine regularly.

How long will tryptophan take to work?

It may take two weeks or more before tryptophan starts to have any effect on your mood, and a further three or four weeks for this effect to reach its maximum. If it has not started working in about six weeks, it is unlikely to work. Unfortunately, in some people, the effect may take a little longer to occur, e.g. several months if you are older.

For how long will I need to keep taking tryptophan?

This should be discussed with your doctor, as people's responses are different. Some people may need to continue taking tryptophan for months or even years. It is usually necessary to take it for several months after you have recovered. Usually, it is best taken for at least 6–12 months to make sure you are fully recovered from your illness. If you have been depressed more than once, it is advisable to continue taking an antidepressant for several years, as this will reduce the chances of the illness recurring.

Is tryptophan addictive?

Tryptophan is not addictive.

Can I stop taking tryptophan suddenly?

Although you should not suffer any withdrawal effects, it is unwise to stop taking tryptophan suddenly, even if you feel better. For it to continue working, tryptophan must be taken every day. If you stop taking it before your doctor advises you to, your symptoms could return.

What should I do if I forget to take a dose?

Start again as soon as you remember, unless it is almost time for your next dose, then go on as before. Do not try to catch up by taking two or more doses at once, as you may experience more side-effects. You should tell your doctor about this at your next appointment. If you have problems remembering your doses (as many people do), ask your pharmacist, doctor, or nurse about this. There are special boxes and devices available that can be used to help you remember.

What sort of side-effects might occur?

Side-effects are rare, but occasionally symptoms, such as nausea (a feeling of sickness), drowsiness, headache, and light-headedness can occur. These tend to wear off after a few days. If they do not or cause you discomfort, you should discuss this with your doctor. It may be possible to adjust your dose to reduce these effects. Taking your tryptophan after food can help to reduce the incidence of nausea. It is not thought that the drug has any major long-term side-effects.

In America early in the 1990s, there were some serious, unpleasant side-effects with health food products that contained tryptophan. Your tablets contain tryptophan, but are not directly linked with these side-effects. It is safest, however, to ensure that your blood is checked regularly, every two months for the first six months, then every six months. Also, if you suffer any severe joint or muscle pain, skin rash, swelling, or fever please tell your doctor immediately.

Will tryptophan make me drowsy?

Tryptophan may make you feel drowsy. You should not drive (see below) or operate machinery until you know how it affects you. You should take extra care, as it may affect your reaction times. It is not, however, a sleeping tablet, although if you take it at night it may help you to sleep.

Will tryptophan cause weight gain?

It is not thought that tryptophan causes any changes in weight. However, if you do start to have problems with your weight tell your doctor at your next appointment, as he/she can arrange for you to see a dietician for advice.

Will tryptophan affect my sex life?

Drugs can affect desire (libido), arousal (erection), and orgasmic ability. Tryptophan is not thought to significantly affect any of these.

Can I drink alcohol while I am taking tryptophan?

You should avoid alcohol except in moderation while taking tryptophan, as it may make you feel sleepier. This can be very important if you need to drive or operate machinery, and you must seek advice on this.

Are there any foods or drinks that I should avoid?

You should have no problems with any food or drink other than alcohol (see above).

Will tryptophan affect my other medication?

You should have few problems if you take other medications, although some can occur. Tryptophan can 'interact' with 'MAOIs' and the 'SSRIs' (e.g. citalopram ['Cipramil®'], escitalopram ['Cipralex®'], fluoxetine ['Prozac®'], fluvoxamine ['Faverin®'], paroxetine ['Seroxat®'], sertraline ['Lustral®']), although your doctor should know about these. This does not mean that the drugs cannot be used together, but you may need to follow your doctor's instructions very carefully. Make sure your doctor knows about all the medicines you are taking. Other medicines, e.g. the painkiller, co-proxamol, can cause drowsiness and, when combined with tryptophan, could make you even drowsier. Recently, there has been much concern about the safety of St. John's wort with many drugs. Until more information is available, you should avoid taking St. John's wort when taking tryptophan. You should tell your doctor before starting or stopping these, or any other drugs.

If I am taking a contraceptive pill, will this be affected?

It is not thought that the contraceptive pill is affected by tryptophan.

What if I want to start a family or discover I'm pregnant?

It is important to consider that there will be a risk to you and your child from taking a medicine during pregnancy, but also a possible risk from stopping the medicine, e.g. suffering a relapse. Unfortunately, no decision is risk-free. It will be for you to decide which is the least risk. All we can do here is to help you understand some of the issues, so that you can make an informed decision. For your information, major malformations occur 'spontaneously' in about 2–4% of all pregnancies, even if no drugs are taken. The main problem with medicines is termed 'teratogenicity', i.e. a medicine causing a malformation in the unborn child. A medicine causing teratogenicity is called a 'teratogen'. Since a baby has completed its main development between days 17 and 60 of the pregnancy (the so-called 'first trimester'), these first 2–16 weeks are the main concern. After that, there may be other problems, e.g. some medicines may cause slower growth. The infant may also be affected after birth, e.g. withdrawal effects are possible with some drugs.

If possible, the best option is to plan in advance. If you think you could become pregnant, discuss this with your doctor and it may be possible to switch to medicines thought to carry least risk, and take other risk-reducing steps, e.g. adjusting doses, taking vitamin supplements, etc. If you have just discovered you are pregnant, don't panic, but, if possible, seek advice from your GP within the next few days. He or she may also want to refer you on to someone with more specialist knowledge of your medicine.

Very few medicines have been shown to be completely safe in pregnancy, so no manufacturer or advisor can ever say any medicine is safe. They will usually advise not to take a medicine during pregnancy, unless the benefit is much greater than the risk. In the UK, there is the NTIS (National Teratology Information Service) which offers individual risk assessments. However, their advice should always be used to help you and your doctor decide what is the risk to you and your baby. There is a risk from taking the medicine and a risk should you stop a medicine, e.g. you might become ill again and need to go back on the medication. The advice offered here is just that—**advice**, but may give you some idea about the possible risks and what (at the time of writing) is known through the medical press.

It may be helpful to know that in the USA, the FDA (Federal Drug Administration) classifies medicines in pregnancy in five groups:

A =	Studies show no risk, so harm to the unborn child appears only a remote possibility
B =	Animal and human studies indicate a lack of risk, but are not fully conclusive
C =	Animal studies indicate a risk, but there is no safety date in humans
D =	A definite risk exists, but the benefit may outweigh the risk in some people
X =	The risk outweighs any possible benefit

Tryptophan is not classified, as it is not available in the USA. Since it is an amino acid (and hence occurs naturally in many foodstuffs) the risk would thus presumably be low, but you should still seek personal advice from your GP, who may then, if necessary, seek further specialist advice.

Will I need a blood test?

You should have one every two to six months.

Can I drive while I am taking tryptophan?

You may feel drowsy when first taking this drug. Until this wears off, or you know how your drug affects you, do not drive or operate machinery. You should take extra care, as it may affect your reaction times.

It is an offence to drive, to attempt to drive, or to be in charge of a vehicle when unfit through drugs. It is advisable to let your insurance company know if you are taking this drug. If you do not and you have an accident, it could affect your insurance cover.

If you are advised by your doctor not to drive, and continue to do so, the General Medical Council has advised doctors to inform the DVLA. The DVLA may then carry out an enquiry.

ST. JOHN'S WORT (Hypericum perforatum)

What is St. John's wort?

St. John's wort (Hypericum perforatum) is one of the oldest known herbal remedies. It has been used for over 2000 years to treat emotional and nervous complaints. It grows throughout Europe, Western Asia and North Africa. In the UK it is a common weed seen by roadsides, on heathland and in woods.

What is St. John's wort used for?

In recent years St. John's wort has become increasingly popular as a herbal alternative to antidepressant drugs, to help improve mood in people who are feeling low or depressed. Research has so far found St. John's wort to be useful in the treatment of mild to moderate depression. It has, however, not been found to be particularly helpful in severe depression. If you are suffering from severe depression you should seek medical advice rather than trying to self medicate.

How does St. John's wort work?

The way in which St. John's wort works to help depression is unclear. It contains at least ten different chemicals that may help improve mood. There are many chemical messengers called monoamines that occur naturally in the brain. If the levels of these monoamines are low then your mood may feel low. St. John's wort may help to stop the breakdown of these monoamines and increase the level back to normal. This helps to improve mood in people who are feeling low or depressed.

How should I take it ?

There are a number of products available on the market containing St. John's wort. When purchasing St. John's wort you should be careful about the potency and purity of the product. Standardised extract (0.3% Hypericum) has been well researched and proven in clinical trials. You should not take St. John's wort if you are:

- Pregnant or breast feeding
- Under 16 years of age

If you are in either of these categories you should speak to your doctor for further advice. There is no evidence that St. John's wort is dangerous as such in pregnancy or breast-feeding, but no evidence that it is safe. So, until further information is available, it should be avoided if you are pregnant or breast-feeding.

When should I take my St. John's wort?

The recommended dose for treating depression is 300mg, taken three times a day.

How long does St. John's wort take to work?

It may take as long as two weeks or more before St. John's wort starts to have any effect on your mood, and a further three or four weeks for this effect to reach its maximum. Unfortunately, in some people, the effect may take even longer to occur, e.g. several months.

For how long will I need to keep taking it?

Some people may need to continue taking it for months or even years. It is usually necessary to take it for at least a month after you have recovered before the dose can be reduced and the medicine eventually stopped. Usually, it is best to take it for at least 6 to 12 months to make sure you are fully over your illness.

Is St. John's wort addictive?

St. John's wort is not thought to be addictive.

Can I stop taking St. John's wort suddenly?

There is no evidence of any problems with stopping St. John's wort suddenly. Although you should not suffer any withdrawal effects, it is unwise to stop taking St. John's wort suddenly, even if you feel better.

What should I do if I forget to take a dose?

If you forget to take a dose, take it as soon as you remember, unless it is time for your next dose. Don't take two doses at once.

What sort of side-effects might occur?

Side effects with St. John's wort are usually rare. However, if you do develop any side effect after taking St. John's wort, stop taking it immediately and, if in any doubt, speak to your doctor or pharmacist.

Will St. John's wort make me drowsy?

Drowsiness is not a main side effect of St. John's wort. If you do feel drowsy, you should not drive (see below) or operate machinery. You should be careful as it may affect your reaction times.

Will St. John's wort cause me to put on weight?

Weight gain is not a reported side effect of St. John's wort. If, however, you do start to have problems with your weight tell your doctor next time you meet as he or she can arrange for you to see a dietician for advice.

What sort of side-effects might occur?

Side-effect	What happens	What to do about it
Common		
Stomach upset	This includes feeling sick and getting diarrhoea (the runs).	If you feel like this for more than a week after starting SJW, tell your doctor.
Confusion	Your mind is all mixed up or confused.	This may happen when you start SJW. If it does not go after a couple of weeks, see your doctor.
Dizziness	Feeling light-headed and faint.	Don't stand up too quickly. Try and lie or sit down if you feel it coming on. Don't drive or operate machinery.
Rare		
Rashes or itching	Blotches, a rash or itching seen anywhere on the body.	Stop taking the SJW and see your doctor now.
Photosensitivity	Getting blotches or blisters in the sun.	This is rare, but known with SJW. Avoid direct sunlight or sun-lamps. Use a high factor sun block cream, e.g. SPF 15 or above.

Table adapted from UK Psychiatric Pharmacy Group leaflets, with kind permission (www.ukppg.org.uk)

Do not worry about this list of side-effects, as you may not experience any. If you experience any unusual symptoms, ask your doctor about these at your next appointment.

Will St. John's wort affect my sex life?

Drugs can affect desire (libido), arousal (erection) and orgasmic ability. St. John's wort is not thought to affect sex life.

Can I drink alcohol while I am taking St. John's wort?

You should avoid alcohol except in moderation while taking St. John's wort as it may make you feel more dizzy or confused. This can be very important if you need to drive or operate machinery and you must seek advice on this.

Are there any foods or drinks that I should avoid ?

You should have no problems with any food or drink other than alcohol (see above).

Will St. John's wort affect my other medication?

St. John's wort can reduce the effectiveness of a number of prescribed medications. If you are prescribed any of the following medications, you should not take St. John's wort without discussion with your doctor:

- Oral contraceptives
- HIV medication
- Warfarin
- Ciclosporin
- Epilepsy treatments
- Migraine treatments
- Digoxin
- Theophylline
- Antidepressants

If you are taking any other medication for any other condition check with your doctor or pharmacist before taking St. John's wort.

If I am taking a contraceptive pill, will this be affected ?

See the answer above.

What if I want to start a family or discover I am pregnant?

It is important to consider that there will be a risk to you and your child from taking a medicine during pregnancy, but also a possible risk from stopping the medicine, e.g. suffering a relapse. Unfortunately, no decision is risk-free. It will be for you to decide which is the least risk. All we can do here is to help you understand some of the issues, so that you can make an informed decision. For your information, major malformations occur 'spontaneously' in about 2–4% of all pregnancies, even if no drugs are taken. The main problem with medicines is termed 'teratogenicity', i.e. a medicine causing a malformation in the unborn child. A medicine causing teratogenicity is called a 'teratogen'. Since a baby has completed its main development between days 17 and 60 of the pregnancy (the so-called 'first trimester'), these first 2–16 weeks are the main concern. After that, there may be other problems, e.g. some medicines may cause slower growth. The infant may also be affected after birth, e.g. withdrawal effects are possible with some drugs.

If possible, the best option is to plan in advance. If you think you could become pregnant, discuss this with your doctor and it may be possible to switch to medicines thought to carry least risk, and take other risk-reducing steps, e.g. adjusting doses, taking vitamin supplements, etc. If you have just discovered you are pregnant, don't panic, but, if possible, seek advice from your GP within the next few days. He or she may also want to refer you on to someone with more specialist knowledge of your medicine.

Very few medicines have been shown to be completely safe in pregnancy, so no manufacturer or advisor can ever say any medicine is safe. They will usually advise not to take a medicine during pregnancy, unless the benefit is much greater than the risk. In the UK, there is the NTIS (National Teratology Information Service) which offers individual risk assessments. However, their advice should always be used to help you and your doctor decide what is the risk to you and your baby. There is a risk from taking the medicine and a risk should you stop a medicine, e.g. you might become ill again and need to go back on the medication. The advice offered here is just that—**advice**, but may give you some idea about the possible risks and what (at the time of writing) is known through the medical press.

It may be helpful to know that in the USA, the FDA (Federal Drug Administration) classifies medicines in pregnancy in five groups:

A =	Studies show no risk, so harm to the unborn child appears only a remote possibility
B =	Animal and human studies indicate a lack of risk, but are not fully conclusive
C =	Animal studies indicate a risk, but there is no safety date in humans
D =	A definite risk exists, but the benefit may outweigh the risk in some people
X =	The risk outweighs any possible benefit

St. John's wort is not classified. Little is known about it in pregnancy so until we know more, St. John's wort is currently best avoided in pregnancy. You should still seek personal advice from your GP, who may then if necessary seek further specialist advice.

Will I need a blood test ?

You should not need to have a blood test to check on your drug, although your doctor may want to check your blood for other reasons.

Can I drive while I am taking St. John's wort?

You may feel dizzy at first when taking St. John's wort. Until this wears off or you know how your drug affects you, do not drive or operate machinery. You should be careful as it may affect your reaction times. It is against the law to drive or attempt to drive when unfit through drugs, or to be in charge of a vehicle when unfit through drugs.

Treatments for epilepsy

Drugs known as anticonvulsants

Drug: Lamotrigine

Drugs available	Brand name(s)	Forms available			
		Tablets	Capsules	Liquid	Injection
Lamotrigine	Lamictal®	✔		✔ (dispersible tablets)	

For what is lamotrigine used?

Lamotrigine is used most often in the treatment of epilepsy, to help control fits or blackouts. It is sometimes used with other antiepileptic drugs, but can be used on its own. There are many other anticonvulsant drugs. It may be necessary to try several drugs in different doses or combinations to find the best therapy for you, i.e. least side-effects and maximum effect.

Lamotrigine is also used to help in depression and as a mood stabiliser to help prevent depression returning when other mood stabilising drugs, such as lithium and carbamazepine, have not helped.

How does lamotrigine work?

Epileptic seizures (fits or blackouts) happen when abnormal electrical discharges (similar to a short circuit causing a spark) occur in the brain. There is a chemical messenger ('neurotransmitter') called glutamate that 'excites' the brain. Lamotrigine may help to decrease the action of the 'excitatory' glutamate. This will help to calm the brain (i.e. make it less 'excited') and reduce the risk of fits occurring, and this same process may explain how it works as a mood stabiliser.

How should I take it?

The tablets should be swallowed with at least half a glass of water while sitting or standing, so that they reach the stomach and do not stick in the throat. The dispersible lamotrigine tablets should be put into a glass of water, stirred with a spoon, and the mixture swallowed when the tablet has dissolved.

When should I take it?

Take it as directed on the medicine label, usually at breakfast and at bedtime. It is particularly important to take this drug regularly each day, as directed by your doctor, to make sure that you are achieving the most effective control of your illness from your lamotrigine.

How long will lamotrigine take to work?

Lamotrigine should begin to work soon after you start taking it if for epilepsy, a bit longer if taking it as a mood stabiliser. It may, however, take some time for your doctor to achieve the right dose for you, and you will need to increase your dose gradually over several weeks (to reduce the chance of getting a skin rash).

For how long will I need to keep taking lamotrigine?

Lamotrigine is a 'preventative medicine' and so will usually need to be taken for a long time. It is important that you keep taking this medication until your doctor tells you to stop. Do not stop taking it just because you feel better. If you stop it before you are advised to do so, your condition may well deteriorate.

Can I stop taking lamotrigine suddenly?

If taking it for epilepsy, you should not stop taking this medication suddenly or without advice from your doctor, as this may cause an increase in fits or blackouts. If your doctor decides that you no longer require the drug, it will be withdrawn gradually (as is any treatment for epilepsy) to make sure that your fits do not return. This is usually by a slight reduction in your dose every few weeks. You should not then experience any problems.

What sort of side-effects might occur?

Side effect	What happens	What to do about it
Common		
Drowsiness	You feel sleepy or sluggish. It can last for a few hours after taking your dose or longer	Do not drive or use machinery. Discuss with your doctor if you can take the drug at a different time of the day
Dizziness	Feeling light-headed and faint	Do not stand up too quickly. Try and lie or sit down if you start feeling dizzy. Do not drive
Headache	Your head is pounding and painful	Try aspirin or paracetamol. Your pharmacist will be able to advise if these are safe to take with other drugs you may be taking
Nausea	Feeling sick	If it is severe, contact your doctor
Uncommon		
Oedema	Swelling in the legs, face, lips, or tongue	Call your doctor now
Skin rashes	Blotches seen anywhere	Stop taking and contact your doctor now
Blurred vision	Things look fuzzy and you cannot focus properly	Do not drive. See your doctor if you are worried. You will not need glasses
Rare		
Seizures	Having a fit or convulsion, or a worsening of your symptoms	Contact your doctor immediately

Table adapted from UK Psychiatric Pharmacy Group leaflets, with kind permission (www.ukppg.org.uk)

Do not worry about this list of side-effects, as you may not experience any. There are other rare side-effects. If you develop any unusual symptoms, ask your doctor about these at your next appointment.

What should I do if I forget to take a dose?

Start again as soon as you remember unless it is almost time for your next dose, then go on as before. Do not try to catch up by taking two or more doses at once, as you may experience more side-effects. You should tell your doctor about this at your next appointment. If you are ill and vomit your tablets, you should take that dose again. The amount in your bloodstream may drop below the level needed to control your fits.

If you have problems remembering your doses (as many people do), ask your pharmacist, doctor, or nurse about this. There are special packs, boxes, and devices available that can be used to help you remember.

Will lamotrigine make me drowsy?

You may feel sleepy, so you must take care if you are allowed to drive or when operating any type of machinery. This effect should wear off or at least reduce after you have been taking it for a while.

Will lamotrigine cause weight gain?

It is not thought that lamotrigine causes any changes in weight. However, if you do start to have problems with your weight, tell your doctor at your next appointment and he/she can arrange for you to see a dietician for advice.

Is lamotrigine addictive?

Lamotrigine is not thought to be habit forming.

Will lamotrigine affect my sex life?

Drugs can affect desire (libido), arousal (erection), and orgasmic ability. Lamotrigine is not thought to affect these significantly, although in rare cases improvement in desire or libido has been reported.

Can I drink alcohol while I am taking lamotrigine?

You should avoid alcohol while taking lamotrigine as it may make you feel sleepier. This is particularly important if you are allowed to drive or operate machinery, and you must seek advice on this.

Are there any foods or drinks that I should avoid?

You should have no problems with any food or drink other than alcohol (see above).

Will lamotrigine affect my other medication?

Tell your doctor about medicines that you may be taking and also before starting or stopping any other drugs. Lamotrigine may interact with valproate ('Epilim®', Convulex®', Depakote®') and carbamazepine (Tegretol®), so your dose will need to be chosen carefully. This does not necessarily mean that the drugs cannot be used together, but you may need to follow your doctor's instructions very carefully.

If I am taking a contraceptive pill, will this be affected?

There should be no problem with lamotrigine.

What if I want to start a family or discover I'm pregnant?

It is important to consider that there will be a risk to you and your child from taking a medicine during pregnancy, but also a possible risk from stopping the medicine, e.g. suffering a relapse. Unfortunately, no decision is risk-free. It will be for you to decide which is the least risk. All we can do here is to help you understand some of the issues, so that you can make an informed decision. For your information, major malformations occur 'spontaneously in about 2–4% of all pregnancies, even if no drugs are taken. The main problem with medicines is termed 'teratogenicity', i.e. a medicine causing a malformation in the unborn child. A medicine causing teratogenicity is called a teratogen'. Since a baby has completed its main development between days 17 and 60 of the pregnancy (the so-called first 'trimester'), these first 2–16 weeks are the main concern. After that, there may be other problems, e.g. some medicines may cause slower growth. The infant may also be affected after birth, e.g. withdrawal effects are possible with some drugs.

If possible, the best option is to plan in advance. If you think you could become pregnant, discuss this with your doctor and it may be possible to switch to medicines thought to carry least risk, and take other risk-reducing steps, e.g. adjusting doses, taking vitamin supplements, etc. If you have just discovered you are pregnant, don't panic, but, if possible, seek advice from your GP within the next few days. He or she may also want to refer you on to someone with more specialist knowledge of your medicine.

Very few medicines have been shown to be completely safe in pregnancy, so no manufacturer or advisor can ever say any medicine is safe. They will usually advise not to take a medicine during pregnancy, unless the benefit is much greater than the risk. In the UK, there is the NTIS (National Teratology Information Service) which offers individual risk assessments. However, its advice should always be used to help you and your doctor decide what is the risk to you and your baby. There is a risk from taking the medicine and a risk should you stop a medicine, e.g. you might become ill again and need to go back on the medication. The advice offered here is just that—**advice**, but may give you some idea about the possible risks and what (at the time of writing) is known through the medical press.

It may be helpful to know that in the USA, the FDA (Federal Drug Administration) classifies medicines in pregnancy in five groups:

A =	Studies show no risk, so harm to the unborn child appears only a remote possibility
B =	Animal and human studies indicate a lack of risk, but are not fully conclusive
C =	Animal studies indicate a risk, but there is no safety date in humans
D =	A definite risk exists, but the benefit may outweigh the risk in some people
X =	The risk outweighs any possible benefit

Lamotrigine is classified as 'C'. There is no evidence of a teratogenic effect, but there is little information available at present and so you should seek personal advice from your GP, who may then, if necessary, seek further specialist advice. If you are taking this medicine for epilepsy, then you will also need to consider the risk of seizures.

Will I need blood tests?

You should not need blood tests with lamotrigine.

Can I drive while taking lamotrigine?

People suffering from epilepsy may drive a motor vehicle (but not a heavy goods vehicle) provided they have been free from fits for one year, or if they have only had fits in their sleep for three years. You should consult your doctor about driving.

It is essential that you report epilepsy, as well as sudden disabling attacks of loss, or partial loss of consciousness, to the 'Driver and Vehicle Licensing Centre' (DVLC). The DVLC will then make a medical assessment of your condition, consulting with your doctor(s) where necessary. For more information see leaflet 'D100' ('*What you need to know about driving licensing*'), which is available from most post offices, or contact the Driver Enquiry Unit, DVLC, SWANSEA SA6 7JL. (Telephone: 01792 772134 between 8.15am. to 4.30pm. on Monday to Friday). You will need to quote your driver number whether you write or telephone. Alternatively, visit the DVLA Website, page:

www.dvla.gov.uk/at_a_glance/content.htm.

If you are allowed to drive, remember that lamotrigine can make you drowsy when you first start taking it, and cause difficulty in concentrating. You must take extra care when driving or operating any type of machinery. It is advisable to let your insurance company know if you are taking these drugs. If you do not and you have an accident, it could affect your insurance cover.

If you are advised by your doctor not to drive, and continue to do so, the General Medical Council has advised doctors to inform the DVLA. The DVLA may then carry out an enquiry.

Drug: Gabapentin

Drugs available	Brand name(s)	Forms available			
		Tablets	Capsules	Liquid	Injection
Gabapentin	Neurontin®		✔		

For what is gabapentin used?

Gabapentin is used to help in the treatment of various types of epilepsy, to control the fits or blackouts. It is nearly always used with other antiepileptic drugs. Gabapentin has also been used as a mood stabiliser where other mood stabilisers have not worked.

How does gabapentin work?

Epileptic seizures (fits or blackouts) happen when abnormal electrical discharges (similar to a short circuit causing a spark) occur in the brain. There is a chemical messenger ('neurotransmitter') called GABA that is 'inhibitory' on the brain and slows it down. In some people it is thought that there may not be high enough levels of GABA and that this helps to 'trigger' fits. Nobody is sure how gabapentin works in epilepsy, but it may increase the action of GABA in the brain, thus helping to reduce the risk of fits.

How should I take it?

The capsules should be swallowed with at least half a glass of water while sitting or standing, so that they reach the stomach and do not stick in the throat.

When should I take it?

Take it as directed on the medicine label, usually at breakfast, mid-afternoon, and bedtime. It is particularly important to take the doses regularly each day as directed by your doctor to make sure that you are achieving the best control of your illness from your medicine. Do not go for more than 12 hours without taking a dose.

How long will gabapentin take to work?

Gabapentin should begin to work soon after you start taking it. However, it may take some time before your doctor finds the right dose for you, and this will probably be increased gradually over several days or weeks.

For how long will I need to keep taking gabapentin?

Gabapentin is a 'preventative medicine' and usually needs to be taken for a long time. It is important that you keep taking this medication until your doctor tells you to stop. Do not stop taking it just because you feel better. If you stop taking it before you are advised to do so, your condition may deteriorate.

Is gabapentin addictive?

Gabapentin is not thought to be habit forming.

Can I stop taking gabapentin suddenly?

You should never stop taking this medication suddenly or without advice from your doctor, as this may cause an increase in fits or blackouts. If your doctor decides that you no longer require this medication, the drug will be withdrawn gradually (as is any treatment for epilepsy), to ensure that your fits do not return. This is usually by a slight reduction in your dose every few weeks. You should not then experience any problems.

What sort of side-effects might occur?

Side-effect	What happens	What to do about it
Common		
Drowsiness	You feel sleepy or sluggish the next morning	Do not drive or use machinery. This should wear off after a few weeks. If it does not, discuss with your doctor—it may be possible to adjust the dose
Dizziness	Feeling light-headed and faint	Do not stand up too quickly. Try and lie or sit down if you start feeling dizzy. Do not drive
Lethargy	You feel tired all the time and do not feel like doing anything	Your dose may be too high. Contact your doctor to discuss this
Blurred vision	Things look fuzzy and you cannot focus properly	Do not drive. If you are worried, see your doctor who may be able to adjust your dose. You will not need glasses
Stomach upset	This includes feeling and being sick and indigestion	If it lasts for more than a week, see your doctor. Your pharmacist may be able to help by giving you something for indigestion
Tremors	Feeling shaky	It is not dangerous. If it troubles you, contact your doctor
Uncommon		
Weight gain	Eating more and putting on weight	A diet high in vegetables and fibre may help prevent weight gain. See also a separate question in this section
Sore throat	Sore throat or cough	This should wear off. If not, mention it to your doctor at your next appointment
Stammer	Stuttering or stammer	This should wear off. If not, mention it to your doctor at your next appointment
Anxiety	Feeling tense or nervous	This should wear off. If not, mention it to your doctor at your next appointment

Table adapted from UK Psychiatric Pharmacy Group leaflets, with kind permission (www.ukppg.org.uk)

Do not worry about this list of side-effects, as you may not experience any. There are other rare side-effects. If you develop any unusual symptoms, ask your doctor about these at your next appointment.

What should I do if I forget to take a dose?

Start again as soon as you remember unless it is almost time for your next dose, then go on as before. Do not try to catch up by taking two or more doses at once as you are at risk of experiencing an increase in the side-effects. You should tell your doctor about this at your next appointment. If you are ill and vomit your tablets, you should take that dose again. Missing a dose or leaving more than 12 hours between doses can cause your fits to return. The amount in your bloodstream may drop below the level needed to control your fits.

If you have problems remembering your doses (as many people do), ask your pharmacist, doctor, or nurse about this. There are special packs, boxes, and devices available that can be used to help you to remember.

Will gabapentin make me drowsy?

You may feel sleepy, so take care if you are allowed to drive or when operating any type of machinery. This effect should wear off or at least reduce after you have been taking it for a while.

Will gabapentin cause weight gain?

About one in twenty people taking gabapentin experience an increase in weight. If you do have problems with weight gain, tell your doctor at your next appointment and he/she can arrange for you to see a dietician for advice.

Will gabapentin affect my sex life?

Drugs can affect desire (libido), arousal (erection), and orgasmic ability. Gabapentin is not thought to have a significant effect on any of these.

Can I drink alcohol while I am taking gabapentin?

You should avoid alcohol while taking gabapentin, as it may make you feel sleepier. This is particularly important if you are allowed to drive or operate machinery, and you must seek advice on this.

Are there any foods or drinks that I should avoid?

You should have no problems with any food or drink other than alcohol (see above).

Will gabapentin affect my other medication?

Gabapentin is not thought to interact significantly with any drugs and you should not experience any problems, although your doses may have to be assessed carefully.

If I am taking a contraceptive pill, will this be affected?

It is not thought that there are any problems with 'the pill' and gabapentin, unlike many other antiepileptic drugs.

What if I want to start a family or discover I'm pregnant?

It is important to consider that there will be a risk to you and your child from taking a medicine during pregnancy, but also a possible risk from stopping the medicine, e.g. suffering a relapse. Unfortunately, no decision is risk-free. It will be for you to decide which is the least risk. All we can do here is to help you understand some of the issues, so you can make an informed decision. For your information, major malformations occur 'spontaneously' in about 2–4% of all pregnancies, even if no drugs are taken. The main problem with medicines is termed 'teratogenicity', i.e. a medicine causing a malformation in the unborn child. A medicine causing teratogenicity is called a 'teratogen'. Since a baby has completed its main development between days 17 and 60 of the pregnancy (the so-called 'first trimester'), these first 2–16 weeks are the main concern. After that, there may be other problems, e.g. some medicines may cause slower growth. The infant may also be affected after birth, e.g. withdrawal effects are possible with some drugs.

If possible, the best option is to plan in advance. If you think you could become pregnant, discuss this with your doctor and it may be possible to switch to medicines thought to carry least risk, and take other risk-reducing steps, e.g.

adjusting doses, taking vitamin supplements, etc. If you have just discovered you are pregnant, don't panic, but, if possible, seek advice from your GP within the next few days. He or she may also want to refer you on to someone with more specialist knowledge of your medicine.

Very few medicines have been shown to be completely safe in pregnancy, so no manufacturer or advisor can ever say any medicine is safe. They will usually advise not to take a medicine during pregnancy, unless the benefit is much greater than the risk. In the UK, there is the NTIS (National Teratology Information Service) which offers individual risk assessments. However, its advice should always be used to help you and your doctor decide what is the risk to you and your baby. There is a risk from taking the medicine and a risk should you stop a medicine, e.g. you might become ill again and need to go back on the medication. The advice offered here is just that—**advice**, but may give you some idea about the possible risks and what (at the time of writing) is known through the medical press.

It may be helpful to know that in the USA, the FDA (Federal Drug Administration) classifies medicines in pregnancy in five groups:

A =	Studies show no risk, so harm to the unborn child appears only a remote possibility
B =	Animal and human studies indicate a lack of risk, but are not fully conclusive
C =	Animal studies indicate a risk, but there is no safety date in humans
D =	A definite risk exists, but the benefit may outweigh the risk in some people
X =	The risk outweighs any possible benefit

Gabapentin is classified as 'C', but there is little human information available at present and so you should seek personal advice from your GP, who may then, if necessary, seek further specialist advice. If you are taking this medicine for epilepsy, then you will also need to consider the risk of seizures.

Will I need blood tests?
You should not need blood tests with gabapentin.

Can I drive while taking gabapentin?
People suffering from epilepsy may drive a motor vehicle (but not a heavy goods vehicle) provided they have been free from fits for one year or if they have only had fits in their sleep for three years. You should consult your doctor about driving.

It is essential that you report epilepsy, as well as sudden disabling attacks of loss or partial loss of consciousness, to the 'Driver and Vehicle Licensing Centre' (DVLC). The DVLC will then make a medical assessment of your condition, consulting with your doctor(s) where necessary. For more information see leaflet "D100' (*'What you need to know about driving licensing'*), which is available from most post offices, or contact the Driver Enquiry Unit, DVLC, SWANSEA SA6 7JL. (Telephone: 01792 772134 between 8.15am. to 4.30pm. Monday to Friday). You will need to quote your driver number whether you write or telephone. Alternatively, visit the DVLA website, page:

www.dvla.gov.uk/at_a_glance/content.htm.

If you are allowed to drive, remember that gabapentin can make you drowsy when you first start taking it, and cause difficulty in concentrating. You must take extra care when driving or operating any type of machinery. It is advisable to let your insurance company know if you are taking this drug. If you do not and you have an accident, it could affect your insurance cover.

If you are advised by your doctor not to drive, and continue to do so, the General Medical Council has advised doctors to inform the DVLA. The DVLA may then carry out an enquiry.

Drugs: Phenobarbital (phenobarbitone) and primidone

Drugs available	Brand name(s)	Forms available			
		Tablets	Capsules	Liquid	Injection
Phenobarbital	Gardenal®	✔		✔	✔
Primidone	Mysoline®	✔			

Phenobarbitone changed its name to phenobarbital in 1998, although both names are still in use. Primidone was nearly taken off the market in 2003, but now will be available until at least 2006.

What are they used for?

Phenobarbital and primidone are mainly used in the treatment of epilepsy to help control fits or blackouts. Primidone is very similar to phenobarbital and in this section all the comments about phenobarbital also apply to primidone. There are many other anticonvulsant drugs. It may be necessary to try several drugs in different doses or combinations to find the best therapy for you, i.e. the least side-effects and maximum effect.

How does phenobarbital work?

Epileptic seizures (fits or blackouts) happen when abnormal electrical discharges (similar to a short circuit causing a spark) occur in the brain. Phenobarbital reduces the risks of these discharges happening by slowing or sedating parts of the brain. This helps to prevent the epileptic seizures. Unfortunately, it may also make some people feel sleepy.

How should I take it?

Tablets:

The tablets should be swallowed with at least half a glass of water while sitting or standing, so that they reach the stomach and do not stick in the throat.

When you collect your tablets from the hospital pharmacy or your local chemist check that your tablets look the same as those you had before; if they do not, ask your pharmacist or dispenser to double check. Some tablets contain a different dose of the same drug.

Liquid:

Phenobarbital is available as an elixir. Your pharmacist should give you a medicine spoon or oral syringe. Use it carefully to measure the correct amount. Ask your pharmacist for a medicine spoon if you do not have one.

If it is necessary for you to have an injection, it will be given by a nurse or doctor.

When should I take it?

Take it as directed on the medicine label. It is particularly important to take the drug regularly each day, as directed by your doctor, to ensure that you are achieving the most effective control of the illness from your medicine.

How long will it take to work?

Phenobarbital should begin to work soon after you start taking it. However, it may take time before your doctor finds the dose that is right for you. It is necessary to achieve a level where the amount of medicine in your blood is high enough to prevent or reduce fits, but low enough to cause the least number of side-effects. Do not attempt to make any changes yourself.

For how long will I need to keep taking it?

Phenobarbital is a 'preventative medicine' and usually needs to be taken for a long time. It is important that you keep taking this medication until your doctor tells you to stop. Do not stop taking it just because you feel better. If you stop before you are advised to do so, your condition may deteriorate.

Is it addictive?

Phenobarbital can be habit forming, but this is unusual in people taking it to prevent fits. If, however, you have been taking phenobarbital for some time, you should not stop taking it suddenly. If you do your fits may recur and you may experience withdrawal symptoms, such as hallucinations, agitation, or sleeplessness (see below).

Can I stop taking it suddenly?

You should never stop taking this medication suddenly or without advice from your doctor, as this may cause an increase in fits or blackouts. Phenobarbital will nearly always need to be withdrawn slowly. If your doctor decides that you no longer require this drug, it will be withdrawn gradually (as is any treatment for epilepsy) to ensure that your fits do not return. This is usually by a slight reduction in dose every few weeks. You should not then experience any problems. If you do develop withdrawal symptoms of hallucinations, agitation, or difficulty in sleeping after stopping treatment, contact your doctor straight away.

What should I do if I forget to take it?

Start again as soon as you remember unless it is almost time for your next dose, then go on as before. Do not try to catch up by taking two or more doses at once, as you may experience an increase in side-effects. You should tell your doctor about this at your next appointment. If you are ill and vomit your tablets you should take that dose again. Missing a dose can cause your fits to return. The amount in your bloodstream may drop below the level needed to control your fits.

If you have problems remembering your doses (as many people do) ask your pharmacist, doctor, or nurse about this. There are special packs, boxes, and devices available that can be used to help you remember.

Will it make me drowsy?

You may feel sleepy and you must take extra care if you are allowed to drive or when operating any type of machinery. This effect should wear off or at least reduce after you have been taking the drug for a while.

Will it cause weight gain?

It is not thought that phenobarbital causes any changes in weight. If, however, you do start to have weight related problems, tell your doctor at your next appointment and he/she can arrange for you to see a dietician for advice.

Will it affect my sex life?

Drugs can affect desire (libido), arousal (erection), and orgasmic ability. The barbiturates are not thought to significantly effect arousal and orgasm, although sedation and drowsiness may have an effect on arousal.

What sort of side-effects might occur?

Side-effect	What happens	What to do about it
Common		
Drowsiness	You feel sleepy or sluggish the next morning	This should wear off after a few weeks. Do not drive or use machinery. If it does not wear off, discuss with your doctor—it may be better to adjust the dose or try a different drug
Fatigue	You feel tired all the time	This may happen early on in treatment and should go away. If you feel like this for more than a week after starting the drug, tell your doctor. It may be possible to adjust your dose slightly
Ataxia	Being very unsteady on your feet	Your phenobarbital blood level may be too high. Contact your doctor now. A blood test may be needed
Depression	Feeling low	Your phenobarbital blood level may be too high. Contact your doctor now. A blood test may be needed
Rare		
Skin rashes	Blotches seen anywhere	You may be allergic to the drug. Do not stop taking the drug (you fits could recur), but see your doctor now

Table adapted from UK Psychiatric Pharmacy Group leaflets, with kind permission (www.ukppg.org.uk)

Do not worry about this list of side-effects, as you may not experience any. There are other rare side-effects. If you develop any unusual symptoms, ask your doctor about these at your next appointment.

Can I drink alcohol while I am taking it?

You should avoid alcohol while taking phenobarbital, as it may make you feel sleepier. This is particularly important if you are allowed to drive or operate machinery, and you must seek advice on this.

Are there any foods or drinks that I should avoid?

You should have no problems with any food or drink other than alcohol (see above).

Will it affect my other medication?

Tell your doctor about any medicines that you may be taking and also before starting or stopping any other drugs. Phenobarbital is affected by and affects the action of many other drugs. These include: other anticonvulsants, anticoagulants, and treatments for asthma and depression. This does not necessarily mean the drugs cannot be used together, but you will need to follow your doctor's instructions very carefully.

You should also consult your pharmacist before buying any medicines over the counter.

If I am taking a contraceptive pill, will this be affected?

It is important that you let your doctor know if you are taking a contraceptive pill because phenobarbital makes 'the pill' less effective and your doctor may need to change you to a higher dose pill. Even with this change, the contraceptive pill may still be less effective. You may want to consider other methods of contraception, e.g. condom or coil. Ask your doctor, or visit your local family planning clinic for advice.

What if I want to start a family or discover I'm pregnant?

It is important to consider that there will be a risk to you and your child from taking a medicine during pregnancy, but also a possible risk from stopping the medicine, e.g. suffering a relapse. Unfortunately, no decision is risk-free. It will be for you to decide which is the least risk. All we can do here is to help you understand some of the issues, so you can make an informed decision. For your information, major malformations occur 'spontaneously' in about 2–4% of all pregnancies, even if no drugs are taken. The main problem with medicines is termed 'teratogenicity', i.e. a medicine causing a malformation in the unborn child. A medicine causing teratogenicity is called a 'teratogen'. Since a baby has completed its main development between days 17 and 60 of the pregnancy (the so-called 'first trimester'), these first 2–16 weeks are the main concern. After that, there may be other problems, e.g. some medicines may cause slower growth. The infant may also be affected after birth, e.g. withdrawal effects are possible with some drugs.

If possible, the best option is to plan in advance. If you think you could become pregnant, discuss this with your doctor and it may be possible to switch to medicines thought to carry least risk, and take other risk-reducing steps, e.g. adjusting doses, taking vitamin supplements, etc. If you have just discovered you are pregnant, don't panic, but, if possible, seek advice from your GP within the next few days. He or she may also want to refer you on to someone with more specialist knowledge of your medicine.

Very few medicines have been shown to be completely safe in pregnancy, so no manufacturer or advisor can ever say any medicine is safe. They will usually advise not to take a medicine during pregnancy, unless the benefit is much greater than the risk. In the UK, there is the NTIS (National Teratology Information Service) which offers individual risk assessments. However, its advice should always be used to help you and your doctor decide what is the risk to you and your baby. There is a risk from taking the medicine and a risk should you stop a medicine, e.g. you might become ill again and need to go back on the medication. The advice offered here is just that—**advice**, but may give you some idea about the possible risks and what (at the time of writing) is known through the medical press.

It may be helpful to know that in the USA, the FDA (Federal Drug Administration) classifies medicines in pregnancy in five groups:

A =	Studies show no risk, so harm to the unborn child appears only a remote possibility
B =	Animal and human studies indicate a lack of risk, but are not fully conclusive
C =	Animal studies indicate a risk, but there is no safety date in humans
D =	A definite risk exists, but the benefit may outweigh the risk in some people
X =	The risk outweighs any possible benefit

Phenobarbitone is classified as 'D'. There are many possible problems associated with phenobarbitone in pregnancy and so you will need to seek personal advice from your GP, who may then, if necessary, seek further specialist advice.

Will I need blood tests?

You will probably have blood tests every few weeks after you start on phenobarbital or primidone. Later, you should make sure that you have a blood test every six months, to ensure that the dose of your medication is enough and not too much for you. It will also check that the drug is not having any adverse effects on your blood. You may need to have extra blood tests if your dose is changed, or if any other drugs you take are changed.

Can I drive while taking phenobarbital?

People suffering from epilepsy may drive a motor vehicle (but not a heavy goods vehicle) provided they have been free from fits for one year, or if they have only had fits in their sleep for three years. You should consult your doctor about driving.

It is essential that you report epilepsy, as well as sudden disabling attacks of loss or partial loss of consciousness, to the 'Driver and Vehicle Licensing Centre' (DVLC). The DVLC will then make a medical assessment of your condition, consulting with your doctor(s) where necessary. For more information see leaflet 'D100' ('*What you need to know about driving licensing*'), which is available from most post offices, or contact the Driver Enquiry Unit, DVLC, SWANSEA SA6 7JL. (Telephone: 01792 772134 between 8.15am to 4.30pm Monday to Friday). You will need to quote your driver number whether you write or telephone. Alternatively, visit the DVLA Website, page:

www.dvla.gov.uk/at_a_glance/content.htm.

If you are allowed to drive, remember that phenobarbital can make you drowsy when you first start taking it, and cause difficulty in concentration. You must take extra care when driving or operating any type of machinery.

It is advisable to let your insurance company know if you are taking this drug. If you do not and you have an accident, it could affect your insurance cover.

If you are advised by your doctor not to drive, and continue to do so, the General Medical Council has advised doctors to inform the DVLA. The DVLA may then carry out an enquiry.

Drug: Phenytoin

Drugs available	Brand name(s)	Forms available			
		Tablets	Capsules	Liquid	Injection
Phenytoin	Epanutin®	✔	✔	✔	✔

Phenytoin is also available as chewable tablets.

For what is phenytoin used?

Phenytoin is mainly used in the treatment of epilepsy to help control fits or blackouts. There are many other anticonvulsant drugs. It may be necessary to try several drugs in different doses or combinations to find the best therapy for you, i.e. the least side-effects and maximum effect. Phenytoin is also occasionally used to relieve the symptoms of trigeminal neuralgia (a painful condition of the face), and some other conditions.

How does phenytoin work?

Epileptic seizures (fits or blackouts) happen when abnormal electrical discharges (similar to a short circuit causing a spark) occur in the brain. Phenytoin reduces the risk of these discharges happening by slowing or sedating parts of the brain, thus helping to prevent the epileptic seizures. Unfortunately, it can also make people feel sleepy.

How should I take it?

Tablets and capsules:

Phenytoin tablets and capsules should be swallowed whole with about a half a glass of water while sitting or standing, so that they reach the stomach and do not stick in the throat. A drink, such as fruit juice, tea, or coffee could be used instead of water.

When you collect your medicine from the pharmacy or doctor's surgery, check that the tablets or capsules look the same as those you had before. If not, ask your pharmacist or dispenser to double check. Some tablets/capsules contain a different dose of the same drug, but look almost the same.

Chewable phenytoin tablets called 'Infatabs®' are also available, but only contain a low dose (50mg) of phenytoin.

Liquids:

Phenytoin is available as a suspension. Your pharmacist should give you a medicine spoon or oral syringes. Use these carefully to measure the correct amount. Ask your pharmacist for a medicine spoon if you do not have one.

You must shake the bottle well before use or the phenytoin will settle to the bottom and cause you to receive too low a dose at the start and too high a dose at the end of the bottle.

If it is necessary for you to have an injection, this will be given by a nurse or doctor.

When should I take my phenytoin?

Take it exactly as directed on the medicine label. If you feel sick or experience a full feeling in your stomach after taking your phenytoin, taking it with or after food helps to reduce this. It is particularly important to take phenytoin regularly, as directed by your doctor, to ensure that you are achieving the most effective control of your illness.

How long will phenytoin take to work?

Phenytoin should begin to work soon after you start taking it. However, it may take time before your doctor finds the dose that is right for you. It is necessary to achieve a level where the amount of medicine in your blood is high enough to prevent or reduce fits, but low enough to cause the least side-effects. Do not attempt to make any changes yourself.

For how long will I need to keep taking phenytoin?

Phenytoin is a 'preventative medicine' and usually needs to be taken for a long time. It is important that you keep taking this medication until your doctor tells you to stop. Do not stop taking it just because you feel better. If you stop before you are advised to do so, your condition may deteriorate.

Is phenytoin addictive?

Phenytoin is not addictive. However, if you have been taking phenytoin for some time, you should not stop taking it suddenly. If you do your fits may recur (see below).

What sort of side-effects might occur?

Side-effect	What happens	What to do about it
Common		
Drowsiness	You feel sleepy or sluggish the next morning	This should wear off after a few weeks. Do not drive or use machinery. If it does not, discuss with your doctor—it may be possible to adjust the dose
Dizziness	Feeling light-headed and faint	Do not stand up too quickly. Try and lie down when you feel it coming on. Do not drive
Ataxia	Being unsteady on your feet	Discuss with your doctor at your next appointment
Nausea	Feeling sick	Take your tablets after food. If nausea is severe, contact your doctor
Sleep disturbances	You cannot sleep very well and may have nightmares	If you feel like this for more than a week after starting the drug, tell your doctor
Headache	Your head is pounding and painful	Try aspirin or paracetamol. Your pharmacist will be able to advise if these are safe to take with other drugs you may be taking
Uncommon		
Low mood	Feeling depressed and lacking interest in activities	Discuss with your doctor at your next appointment. He/she may decide to adjust your drug or dose
Skin rashes	Blotches seen anywhere	You may be allergic to the drug. Do not stop taking the drug (your fits could recur), but see your doctor now
Rare		
Phenytoin toxicity	More hair on the face and body; difficulty remembering things and with concentrating; thickening of the skin	If these happen, discuss with your doctor at your next appointment. A blood test will be needed. Your dose or the drug may need to be changed
Seizure changes	A change in the number or severity of seizures or fits	Let your doctor know as soon as reasonable. A blood test will be needed. Your dose may need to be changed
Gum hypoplasia	Swelling or bleeding of the gums	Careful brushing of your teeth and gums, and regular dental check-ups are necessary. A blood test will be needed. Your dose may need to be changed

Table adapted from UK Psychiatric Pharmacy Group leaflets, with kind permission (www.ukppg.org.uk)

Do not worry about this list of side-effects, as you may not experience any. There are other rare side-effects. If you develop any unusual symptoms, ask your doctor about these at your next appointment.

Can I stop taking phenytoin suddenly?

This is a 'preventative medicine'. Never stop taking phenytoin suddenly or without advice from your doctor, as this could mean an increase in fits or blackouts. Phenytoin nearly always needs to be withdrawn slowly. This is usually done by a slight reduction in your dose every few weeks.

What should I do if I forget to take a dose?

Start again as soon as you remember unless it is almost time for your next dose, then go on as before. Do not try to catch up by taking two or more doses at once, as you may experience an increase in side-effects. If you are ill and vomit after taking your phenytoin, you should take that dose again. You should tell your doctor about either of these at your next appointment. Missing a dose can cause your fits to return. The amount of phenytoin in your blood may drop below the level needed to control your fits.

If you have problems remembering your doses (as many people do) ask your pharmacist, doctor, or nurse about this. There are special packs, boxes, and devices available that can be used to help you remember.

Will phenytoin make me drowsy?

You may feel sleepy to start with. Extra care must be taken if you are allowed to drive or when operating any type of machinery. This effect should wear off or at least reduce after you have been taking phenytoin for a while.

Will phenytoin cause weight gain?

It is not thought that phenytoin causes any changes in weight, but should you start to have weight-related problems, tell your doctor at your next appointment. He/she can arrange for you to see a dietician for advice.

Will it affect my sex life?

Drugs can affect desire (libido), arousal (erection), and orgasmic ability. Phenytoin has not been reported to have a significant effect, although drowsiness and headache may have an effect on desire.

Can I drink alcohol while I am taking phenytoin?

There is no complete ban on drinking alcohol if phenytoin is taken, but make sure you do not have more than one or two drinks a day, as this may decrease the effect of the phenytoin. Some effects of alcohol, such as unsteadiness and drowsiness, may increase if you are taking phenytoin.

Are there any foods or drinks that I should avoid?

You should have no problems with any food or drink other than alcohol (see above).

Will phenytoin affect my other medication?

Many drugs, including other anticonvulsants and antifungals, may affect the phenytoin in your body. As the level of phenytoin in your blood needs to be exact for you, you must tell your doctor before starting or stopping any other drugs. It is probably better to take paracetamol rather than aspirin, as aspirin can occasionally upset phenytoin levels. Phenytoin may also 'interact' with some heart drugs, antibiotics, steroids, and treatments for stomach ulcers and arthritis. This does not necessarily mean the drugs cannot be used together, just that you will need to follow your doctor's instructions very carefully.

If I am taking a contraceptive pill, will this be affected?

It is important that you let your doctor know if you are taking a contraceptive pill because phenytoin makes 'the pill' less effective and your doctor may need to change you to a higher dose pill. Even with this change, the contraceptive pill may still be less effective. You may want to consider other methods of contraception, e.g. condom or coil. Ask your doctor, or visit your local family planning clinic for advice.

What if I want to start a family or discover I'm pregnant?

It is important to consider that there will be a risk to you and your child from taking a medicine during pregnancy, but also a possible risk from stopping the medicine, e.g. suffering a relapse. Unfortunately, no decision is risk-free. It will be for you to decide which is the least risk. All we can do here is to help you understand some of the issues, so you can make an informed decision. For your information, major malformations occur 'spontaneously' in about 2–4% of all pregnancies, even if no drugs are taken. The main problem with medicines is termed 'teratogenicity', i.e. a medicine causing a malformation in the unborn child. A medicine causing teratogenicity is called a 'teratogen'. Since a baby has completed its main development between days 17 and 60 of the pregnancy (the so-called 'first trimester'), these first 2–16 weeks are the main concern. After that, there may be other problems, e.g. some medicines may cause slower growth. The infant may also be affected after birth, e.g. withdrawal effects are possible with some drugs.

If possible, the best option is to plan in advance. If you think you could become pregnant, discuss this with your doctor and it may be possible to switch to medicines thought to carry least risk, and take other risk-reducing steps, e.g. adjusting doses, taking vitamin supplements, etc. If you have just discovered you are pregnant, don't panic, but, if possible, seek advice from your GP within the next few days. He or she may also want to refer you on to someone with more specialist knowledge of your medicine.

Very few medicines have been shown to be completely safe in pregnancy, so no manufacturer or advisor can ever say any medicine is safe. They will usually advise not to take a medicine during pregnancy, unless the benefit is much greater than the risk. In the UK, there is the NTIS (National Teratology Information Service) which offers individual risk assessments. However, its advice should always be used to help you and your doctor decide what is the risk to you and your baby. There is a risk from taking the medicine and a risk should you stop a medicine, e.g. you might become ill again and need to go back on the medication. The advice offered here is just that—**advice**, but may give you some idea about the possible risks and what (at the time of writing) is known through the medical press.

It may be helpful to know that in the USA, the FDA (Federal Drug Administration) classifies medicines in pregnancy in five groups:

A =	Studies show no risk, so harm to the unborn child appears only a remote possibility
B =	Animal and human studies indicate a lack of risk, but are not fully conclusive
C =	Animal studies indicate a risk, but there is no safety date in humans
D =	A definite risk exists, but the benefit may outweigh the risk in some people
X =	The risk outweighs any possible benefit

Phenytoin is classified as 'D'. There are many possible problems associated with phenytoin in pregnancy and so you will need to seek personal advice from your GP, who may then, if necessary, seek further specialist advice. The risks can be reduced by, for example, adjusting doses, and taking folic acid and vitamin supplements before you become pregnant and during pregnancy.

Will I need blood tests?

You will need to have blood tests every few weeks after you start taking phenytoin. Once you have stabilised, you then need to have blood tests every three to six months to ensure that the dose of phenytoin is enough and not too much or too little for you. It is also important to have extra blood tests if you suffer any different or increases in side-effects, your dose is changed, or any other drug you are taking is changed.

Can I drive while taking phenytoin?

People suffering from epilepsy may drive a motor vehicle, but not a heavy goods vehicle, provided they have been free from fits for one year, or if they have only had fits in their sleep for three years. You should consult your doctor about driving.

It is essential that you report epilepsy, as well as sudden disabling attacks of loss or partial loss of consciousness, to the 'Driver and Vehicle Licensing Centre' (DVLC). The DVLC will then make a medical assessment of your condition, consulting with your doctor(s) where necessary. For more information see leaflet 'D100' ('*What you need to know about driving licensing*'), which is available from most post offices, or contact the Driver Enquiry Unit, DVLC, SWANSEA SA6 7JL. (Telephone: 01792 772134 between 8.15am. to 4.30pm. Monday to Friday). You will need to quote your driver number whether you write or telephone. Alternatively, visit the DVLA Website, page:

www.dvla.gov.uk/at_a_glance/content.htm.

If you are allowed to drive, remember that phenytoin can make you drowsy when you first start taking it and cause difficulty in concentrating. You must take extra care when driving or operating any type of machinery.

It is advisable to let your insurance company know if you are taking this drug. If you do not and you have an accident, it could affect your insurance cover.

If you are advised by your doctor not to drive, and continue to do so, the General Medical Council has advised doctors to inform the DVLA. The DVLA may then carry out an enquiry.

Treatments for epilepsy and to help as mood stabilisers

Drugs: Carbamazepine and oxcarbazepine

Drugs available	Brand name(s)	Forms available			
		Tablets	Capsules	Liquid	Injection
Carbamazepine	Tegretol® [1]	✔		✔ (sugar-free)	
	Tegretol Retard®	✔			
Oxcarbazepine	Trileptal®	✔			

1. 'Tegretol®' tablets come as plain tablets, 'sustained release' tablets (Tegretol Retard®) and chewable tablets. Carbamazepine is also available as suppositories.

For what are these drugs used?

Carbamazepine has three main uses:

- it can be used to help prevent mood swings, e.g. feeling 'high' or 'low', in people who suffer from bipolar affective disorder (also called manic-depression). There are also a number of other drugs that are useful in helping to stabilise moods
- it can be used to help control fits or blackouts
- it may be used to relieve the symptoms of trigeminal neuralgia (a painful condition of the face).

Carbamazepine is also used to help a number of other illnesses, such as alcohol withdrawal, alcohol dependence, schizophrenia, and withdrawal from benzodiazepines. Oxcarbazepine is similar and a newer drug also licensed to treat epilepsy. This section mainly refers to carbamazepine, but most of the answers apply to oxcarbazepine as well.

How do they work?

In epilepsy, epileptic seizures (fits or blackouts) happen when abnormal electrical discharges (similar to a short circuit causing a spark) occur in the brain. These drugs reduce the incidences of these discharges, but exactly how they work in people with mood problems is not known. They seem to help stabilise the brain's activity.

How should I take them?

Tablets:

Tablets should be swallowed with at least half a glass of water while sitting or standing, so that they reach the stomach and do not stick in the throat.

'Tegretol Retard®' tablets should be swallowed whole and not chewed. These tablets are made so that the carbamazepine is released over a long period of time. This can help to reduce side-effects, or reduce the number of times a day you need to take the medicine. If you cannot swallow them whole, they can be broken, but do not crush, chew, or dissolve them, as this will cause the drug to be released too soon. 'Tegretol Chewtabs®' are available, which may be chewed or sucked.

Liquids:

Your pharmacist should give you a medicine spoon or an oral syringe. Use it carefully to measure the correct dose. Ask your pharmacist for a medicine spoon if you do not have one. Shake the bottle well before use, as the drug can settle to the bottom, causing you to receive too low a dose at the start and too high a dose at the end of the bottle, which could be dangerous.

When should I take my medication?

Take the dose as directed on the medicine label. You should take it at regular times each day. 'Tegretol Chewtabs®' should be taken with or after food. Taking any of the other tablets or liquid at meal times often makes remembering easier. There are no problems in taking carbamazepine or oxcarbazepine with or after food. If the instructions say take **once** a day, this is usually best at bedtime, as the medication may make you drowsy. However, neither of these drugs are sleeping tablets.

If you are taking the drug to control fits or blackouts, it is particularly important that it is taken regularly, as directed by your doctor, to ensure you are achieving the most effective control. Missing a dose can cause the return of fits.

How long will they take to work?

If you are taking these drugs to help control fits or blackouts, they should begin to work a few weeks after you start taking them. It may be some time before your doctor achieves the right dose for you. The aim is to achieve a level of medicine in your blood that is high enough to prevent or reduce fits, but low enough to cause the least side-effects. Do not attempt to make any changes yourself. If you are taking carbamazepine to help prevent mood swings, it may take several months to reach its maximum benefit.

Are they addictive?

They are not addictive. However, if you are taking them for epilepsy, you should not stop taking them suddenly, as explained below.

Can I stop taking them suddenly?

They are a 'preventative medicine'. If you are taking either drug to help control fits or blackouts never stop taking it suddenly, or without advice from your doctor, as this may cause an increase in your fits. If you are taking it to help prevent mood swings, it is also unwise to stop taking it suddenly, even if you feel better, but you should not get any withdrawal symptoms. For it to continue working effectively, the drug must be taken every day. If you do stop taking it before you are advised to do so by your doctor, your symptoms could return.

What should I do if I forget to take a dose?

Start again as soon as you remember unless it is almost time for your next dose, then go on as before. Do not try to catch up by taking two or more doses at once, as you may experience an increased risk of side-effects. You should tell your doctor about this at your next appointment. If you are taking carbamazepine or oxcarbazepine to help control fits or blackouts, and you are ill and vomit soon after taking your tablets, you should take that dose again. Missing a dose can cause your fits to return. The amount in your blood may drop below the level needed to control your fits.

If you have problems remembering your doses (as many people do) ask your pharmacist, doctor, or nurse about this. There are special packs, boxes, and devices available that can be used to help you remember.

What sort of side-effects might occur?

Side-effect	What happens	What to do about it
Common		
Drowsiness	Feeling sleepy or sluggish. It can last for a few hours after taking your dose	Do not drive or use machinery. Ask your doctor if you can take your tablets at a different time of the day or change to the sustained release (Tegretol Retard®) tablet.
Diplopia	Seeing double or 'double vision'	Do not drive or use machinery. You will not need new glasses, but see your doctor if you are worried. Taking the sustained release tablets (Retard®) may help
Dizziness	Feeling light-headed and faint	Do not stand up too quickly. Try and lie down when you feel it coming on. Do not drive
Stomach upset	Feeling sick and being sick. You may also have a dry mouth	If it is severe, contact your doctor. It may be possible to adjust your dose or when you take the tablets
Uncommon		
Headache	When your head is painful and pounding	Ask your chemist if it is safe to take aspirin or paracetamol. Do not take co-proxamol ('Distalgesic®')
Ataxia	Being very unsteady on your feet	Your carbamazepine level may be too high. Contact your doctor now. A blood test may be needed
Rare		
Constipation	Feeling 'blocked up' inside. You cannot pass a motion	Make sure you eat enough fibre, bran, or fruit and that you are drinking enough fluid. Keep active and take plenty of exercise, e.g. walking. If this does not help, ask your doctor or pharmacist for a mild laxative
Confusion	Your mind is all mixed up	Your carbamazepine level may be too high. Contact your doctor now. A blood test may be needed
Erythematous rash	A red rash seen anywhere on the skin	Stop taking the drug and contact your doctor now. This is less common with oxcarbazepine
Ankle oedema	Swelling on the ankles, legs, or feet	It is not usually dangerous and is less common with carbamazepine. Tell your doctor at your next appointment
'SIADH'—this can lead to hypo-natraemia (low sodium) and water intoxication	Symptoms include: not much urine, headache, confusion, tiredness and, if very severe, seizures and coma	This can be dangerous. Contact your doctor now
Very rare		
Agranulocytosis	Low numbers of white cells in the blood. You may suffer from more infections, bruise more easily, have a persistent sore throat, or a temperature	See your doctor now if you catch an infection, sore throat, fever, or bruise more easily. You may need a blood test. See also a separate question in this section

Table adapted from UK Psychiatric Pharmacy Group leaflets, with kind permission (www.ukppg.org.uk)

Do not worry about this list of side-effects, as you may not experience any. There are other rare side-effects. If you develop any unusual symptoms, ask your doctor about these at your next appointment.

It is not thought that these drugs have any major long-term side-effects, if your dose and blood are monitored with care.

Will these drugs make me drowsy?

They may make you feel a bit drowsy or sleepy at first. You should not drive or operate machinery until you know how they affect you. You should take extra care, as they may affect your reflexes or reaction times. They are not, however, sleeping tablets, although they may help you to sleep if you take them at night.

Will they cause weight gain?

Neither drug is thought to cause changes in weight. However, if you do start to have problems, tell your doctor at your next appointment and he/she can arrange for you to see a dietician for advice.

Will they affect my sex life?

Drugs can affect desire (libido), arousal (erection), and orgasmic ability. Neither drug has been reported to have a major adverse effect on these three stages. However, if this does seem to happen you should discuss it with your doctor, as a change in dose may help to minimise problems.

Can I drink alcohol while I am taking these drugs?

You should avoid alcohol while taking carbamazepine or oxcarbazepine, as they may make you feel sleepier. This is particularly important if you are allowed to drive or operate machinery. Seek advice on this.

Are there any foods or drinks that I should avoid?

You should have no problems with any food or drink other than alcohol (see above).

Will they affect my other medication?

Some drugs affect carbamazepine and oxcarbazepine. Conversely, they also affect the action of some other drugs. Tell your doctor of any medicines that you may be taking and also before starting or stopping other drugs. These other drugs include: some treatments for epilepsy, some antibiotics, anticoagulants, treatments for depression, schizophrenia, oral contraceptives (see below), and some heart conditions. This does not necessarily mean the drugs cannot be used together, just that you will need to follow your doctor's instructions very carefully. You should also talk to your pharmacist before buying any medicines over the counter.

If I am taking a contraceptive pill, will this be affected?

It is important that you let your doctor know if you are taking a contraceptive pill because both these drugs make 'the pill' less effective. Your doctor may need to change you to a higher dose pill. Even with this change, the contraceptive pill may still be less effective. You may want to consider other methods of contraception, e.g. condom or coil. Ask your doctor, or visit your local family planning clinic for advice.

What if I want to start a family or discover I'm pregnant?

It is important to consider that there will be a risk to you and your child from taking a medicine during pregnancy, but also a possible risk from stopping the medicine, e.g. suffering a relapse. Unfortunately, no decision is risk-free. It will be for you to decide which is the least risk. All we can do here is to help you understand some of the issues, so you can make an informed decision. For your information, major malformations occur 'spontaneously' in about 2–4% of all pregnancies, even if no drugs are taken. The main problem with medicines is termed 'teratogenicity', i.e. a medicine causing a malformation in the unborn child. A medicine causing teratogenicity is called a 'teratogen'. Since a baby has completed its main development between days 17 and 60 of the pregnancy (the so-called 'first trimester'), these first 2–16 weeks are the main concern. After that, there may be other problems, e.g. some medicines may cause slower growth. The infant may also be affected after birth, e.g. withdrawal effects are possible with some drugs.

If possible, the best option is to plan in advance. If you think you could become pregnant, discuss this with your doctor and it may be possible to switch to medicines thought to carry least risk, and take other risk-reducing steps, e.g. adjusting doses, taking vitamin supplements, etc. If you have just discovered you are pregnant, don't panic, but, if possible, seek advice from your GP within the next few days. He or she may also want to refer you on to someone with more specialist knowledge of your medicine.

Very few medicines have been shown to be completely safe in pregnancy, so no manufacturer or advisor can ever say any medicine is safe. They will usually advise not to take a medicine during pregnancy, unless the benefit is much greater than the risk. In the UK, there is the NTIS (National Teratology Information Service) which offers individual risk assessments. However, its advice should always be used to help you and your doctor decide what is the risk to you and your baby. There is a risk from taking the medicine and a risk should you stop a medicine, e.g. you might become ill again and need to go back on the medication. The advice offered here is just that—**advice**, but may give you some idea about the possible risks and what (at the time of writing) is known through the medical press.

It may be helpful to know that in the USA, the FDA (Federal Drug Administration) classifies medicines in pregnancy in five groups:

A =	Studies show no risk, so harm to the unborn child appears only a remote possibility
B =	Animal and human studies indicate a lack of risk, but are not fully conclusive
C =	Animal studies indicate a risk, but there is no safety date in humans
D =	A definite risk exists, but the benefit may outweigh the risk in some people
X =	The risk outweighs any possible benefit

Carbamazepine and oxcarbazepine are classified as 'C', but should probably be classified as 'D'. There is some evidence of problems, e.g. a 1 in 100 chance of spina bifida and a 'carbamazepine syndrome'. You will need to seek personal advice from an expert, as counselling and screening is recommended. Taking folic acid supplements before becoming pregnant and throughout pregnancy may reduce this risk. You will also need to consider the risk of relapse if you stop your carbamazepine. If you are taking this medicine for epilepsy, then you will also need to consider the risk of seizures. One bit of good news is that one study was able to show that, over the first few years of life, carbamazepine did not appear to have an effect on the intelligence and speech abilities of children born to mothers who took carbamazepine throughout pregnancy.

Will I need blood tests?

You may need to have several blood tests after starting treatment. You may then need a test every six months to make sure that the dose of your medication is enough, but not too much for you. This is particularly important if you are taking carbamazepine or oxcarbazepine for fits or blackouts. You may also need a test if your dose or tablet is changed, other drugs you are taking are changed, or to check that your drug is not affecting your white blood cells.

Can I drive while taking these drugs?

They can make you drowsy or sleepy, and cause blurred or double vision when you first start taking them. You must take extra care if you are allowed to drive or when operating any type of machinery.

It is essential that you report epilepsy, as well as sudden disabling attacks of loss or partial loss of consciousness, to the 'Driver and Vehicle Licensing Centre' (DVLC). The DVLC will then make a medical assessment of your illness, consulting with your doctor(s) where necessary. For more information see leaflet 'D100' (*What you need to know about driving licensing*'), which is available from most post offices, or contact the Driver Enquiry Unit, DVLC, SWANSEA SA6 7JL. (Telephone: 01792 772134 between 8.15am. and 4.30pm. Monday to Friday). You will need to quote your driver number whether you write or telephone. Alternatively, visit the DVLA Website, page:

www.dvla.gov.uk/at_a_glance/content.htm.

It is also advisable to let your insurance company know if you are taking these drugs. If you do not, and you have an accident, it could affect your insurance cover.

If you are advised by your doctor not to drive, and continue to do so, the General Medical Council has advised doctors to inform the DVLA. The DVLA may then carry out an enquiry.

Drug: Valproate (sodium valproate, valproic acid or semisodium valproate)

Drugs available	Brand name(s)	Forms available			
		Tablets	Capsules	Liquid	Injection
Sodium valproate	Epilim® Epilim Chrono®	✔ ✔		✔	✔
Valproate semisodium	Depakote®	✔			
Valproic acid	Convulex®		✔		

Sodium valproate, valproic acid and semisodium valproate are different forms of the same drug. They are virtually the same and on these pages all the information about valproate applies to valproic acid, sodium valproate and valproate semisodium.

For what is valproate used?

Valproate is generally used in the treatment of epilepsy to help control fits (seizures or blackouts). There are many other drugs that help to treat epilepsy. Valproate can also be used to help mood disorders, such as bipolar affective disorder or manic-depression (especially if the person is 'high'—as an antimanic) and some other illnesses, particularly when other treatments have not been effective.

How does valproate work?

It is not entirely clear how valproate works (either as a mood stabiliser or as an anticonvulsant), as it has several actions in the brain. First, there is a chemical messenger (or 'neurotransmitter') called GABA, which is 'inhibitory', i.e. it calms the brain down. Once it has worked, there are other chemicals (or 'enzymes') that are there to break GABA down so that it can no longer work. In people with normal levels of GABA, this prevents it from reaching levels that are too high. In some people, it is thought that there may not be enough GABA in the brain. This lack seems to 'trigger' fits or over-activity/mania. Valproate helps to stop the breakdown of GABA and so leaves enough to help prevent the fits, blackouts, and over-activity. Secondly, it may inhibit 'repetitive firing' of neurones. When a message is passed, there is a short 'refractory' period or gap before the next message can be passed, during which time the nerve ending resets itself (this takes about one thousandth of a second). Valproate may increase this 'refractory' period by a small amount. Under normal circumstances this makes no difference, but if the brain is overactive and many messages are being passed in quick succession (i.e. when you are feeling high), the effect of the valproate will be to slow the number of messages back to the normal level. For example, if the next message follows before the nerve has reset itself, the message cannot be passed. Valproate may also affect noradrenaline receptors.

How should I take it?

Tablets:

The tablets should be swallowed with at least half a glass of water while sitting or standing, so that they reach your stomach and do not stick in your throat.

It is especially important that you swallow 'enteric coated' tablets or capsules whole (all except the 100mg Epilim®), and do not crush or chew them. The coating helps to prevent the occurrence of stomach upsets. Crushing or chewing causes the drug to be released too soon and you may suffer side-effects. Valproate tablets that are not enteric coated (i.e. Epilim® 100mg) may be crushed if necessary.

Taking fizzy drinks (e.g. colas) with the 100mg tablets and syrups may also lead to stomach upsets. Should this happen, do not drink too many fizzy drinks.

Liquids:

Valproate is available as a syrup and as a sugar-free liquid. Your pharmacist should give you a medicine spoon or oral syringe. Use it carefully to measure the correct amount. Ask your pharmacist for a medicine spoon, if you do not have one.

If it is necessary for you to have an injection, a nurse or doctor will give this.

When should I take my valproate?

Take it as directed on the medicine label. It is better to take valproate after food. It is particularly important to take this regularly, as directed by your doctor, to ensure that you are achieving the most effective control from your medication. Missing a dose can cause fits or symptoms to return.

How long will valproate take to work?

Valproate should begin to work soon after you start taking it. It may, however, take time before your doctor finds the dose that is right for you. The aim is to achieve a level of medicine in your blood that is high enough to prevent or reduce fits, but low enough to cause the least amount of side-effects. Do not attempt to make any changes yourself unless specifically told to do so. If you are taking it to help prevent mood swings, it may take several months to reach maximum effect.

For how long will I need to keep taking valproate?

Valproate is a 'preventative medicine'. It is, therefore, important that you keep taking valproate until your doctor tells you to stop. Do not stop taking it just because you feel better. If you stop before you are advised to do so, your fits or symptoms may worsen (see also *'What should I do if I forget to take a dose'*).

Is valproate addictive?

Valproate is not addictive.

Can I stop taking valproate suddenly?

This is a 'preventative medicine'. Never stop taking this medication suddenly or without advice from your doctor, as this may cause an increase in your fits or blackouts. When the time comes to stop your valproate, this is usually by a slight reduction in your dose every few weeks.

What should I do if I forget to take a dose?

Start again as soon as you remember unless it is almost time for your next dose, then go on as before. Do not try to catch up by taking two or more doses at once, as you may experience an increase in side-effects. You should tell your doctor about this at your next appointment. If you are ill and vomit after taking your valproate, you should take that dose again. You should tell your doctor about either of these at your next appointment. Missing a dose can cause your fits to return. The amount in your blood may drop below the level needed to control your fits.

If you have problems remembering your doses (as many people do) ask your pharmacist, doctor, or nurse about this. There are special packs, boxes, and devices available that can be used to help you remember.

Will valproate make me drowsy?

You may feel sleepy when you first start taking this drug, so you must take extra care if you are allowed to drive or when operating any type of machinery. This effect should wear off after you have been taking it for a while.

Will valproate cause weight gain?

Valproate can make some people feel hungrier and they may put on weight. A few people may put on weight without eating more. If you start to get any weight gain or have other weight-related problems, your doctor can arrange for you to see a dietician for advice.

Will valproate affect my sex life?

Drugs can affect desire (libido), arousal (erection), and orgasmic ability. Valproate is not thought to have a major adverse effect on these three stages. However, if this does seem to happen, you should discuss it with your doctor, as a change in dose may help minimise any problem.

Can I drink alcohol while I am taking valproate?

There is no complete ban on drinking alcohol if you are taking valproate, but make sure you do not have more than one or two drinks a day, as it may make you feel sleepier. This is particularly important if you are allowed to drive or operate machinery, and you must seek advice on this.

Are there any foods, or drinks that I should avoid?

Fizzy drinks (e.g. colas) can cause stomach upsets if taken with the uncoated Epilim® tablets (100mg) or syrup. This does not happen with the other tablets or capsules. Other than this, you should have no problems with any food or drink apart from alcohol (see above).

What sort of side-effects might occur?

Side-effect	What happens	What to do about it
Common		
Increased appetite and weight gain	Eating more and putting on weight	A diet high in vegetables and fibre should help prevent weight gain. See also separate question in this section
Uncommon		
Gastric irritation	You have an upset stomach. This usually happens at the start of treatment	Take your valproate with or after food. If this is severe or does not stop, see your doctor now. This may be less common with Depakote® and the Epilim Chrono® tablets
Hair loss	Some of your hair falls out and may seem thinner. This stops after a while	Discuss with your doctor. This can be upsetting for some people. Sometimes it grows back a little curly
Nausea	Feeling sick	If it is severe, contact your doctor
Rare		
Drowsiness	Feeling sleepy or sluggish. This usually happens early in treatment and should cease	Do not drive or use machinery. Ask your doctor if you can take your valproate at a different time
Impaired liver function	Your liver is not working very well	You may feel sleepy, be sick, lose your appetite, and your skin may look yellow. Stop taking valproate and see your doctor now
Tremor	Feeling shaky	This may be due to the dose of valproate you are taking. Discuss with your doctor
Ataxia	Being very unsteady on your feet	Your valproate dose may be too high. Contact your doctor now
Confusion	Your mind is all mixed up	Your valproate dose may be too high. Contact your doctor now
Lethargy	You feel tired all the time and do not feel like doing anything	Your valproate dose may be too high. Contact your doctor now
Thrombocytopenia and impaired platelet function	Low numbers of platelets in your blood and they may not work very well	You may bruise without reason and bleed easily. Stop taking valproate and see your doctor now
Rash	A rash or itching seen anywhere on the skin	Stop taking your valproate and contact your doctor now

Table adapted from UK Psychiatric Pharmacy Group leaflets, with kind permission (www.ukppg.org.uk)

Do not worry about this list of side-effects, as you may not experience any. There are other rare side-effects. If you develop any unusual symptoms, ask your doctor about these at your next appointment.

Will valproate affect my other medication?

If you are taking enteric-coated tablets or capsules, do not take indigestion remedies at the same time of day. This is because indigestion remedies contain alkalis—substances that can break down the coating of the tablet before it reaches the stomach. You may then experience an increase in side-effects. If you need to take something for indigestion, wait for at least two hours after taking your sodium valproate EC tablets or capsules.

Antidepressants and antipsychotic drugs can decrease the effect of this drug. Make sure your doctor knows if you are taking these, or any other medication and he/she will be able to adjust your medication accordingly. If you have a headache, it is better to take paracetamol rather than aspirin while you are taking valproate. This does not necessarily mean that some of these drugs cannot be used together, just that you may need to follow your doctor's instructions very carefully.

If I am taking a contraceptive pill, will this be affected?

It is not thought that the contraceptive pill is affected by valproate.

What if I want to start a family or discover I'm pregnant?

It is important to consider that there will be a risk to you and your child from taking a medicine during pregnancy, but also a possible risk from stopping the medicine, e.g. suffering a relapse. Unfortunately, no decision is risk-free. It will be for you to decide which is the least risk. All we can do here is to help you understand some of the issues, so you can make an informed decision. For your information, major malformations occur 'spontaneously' in about 2–4% of all pregnancies, even if no drugs are taken. The main problem with medicines is termed 'teratogenicity', i.e. a medicine causing a malformation in the unborn child. A medicine causing teratogenicity is called a 'teratogen'. Since a baby has completed its main development between days 17 and 60 of the pregnancy (the so-called 'first trimester'), these first 2–16 weeks are the main concern. After that, there may be other problems, e.g. some medicines may cause slower growth. The infant may also be affected after birth, e.g. withdrawal effects are possible with some drugs.

If possible, the best option is to plan in advance. If you think you could become pregnant, discuss this with your doctor and it may be possible to switch to medicines thought to carry least risk, and take other risk-reducing steps, e.g. adjusting doses, taking vitamin supplements, etc. If you have just discovered you are pregnant, don't panic, but, if possible, seek advice from your GP within the next few days. He or she may also want to refer you on to someone with more specialist knowledge of your medicine.

Very few medicines have been shown to be completely safe in pregnancy, so no manufacturer or advisor can ever say any medicine is safe. They will usually advise not to take a medicine during pregnancy, unless the benefit is much greater than the risk. In the UK, there is the NTIS (National Teratology Information Service) which offers individual risk assessments. However, its advice should always be used to help you and your doctor decide what is the risk to you and your baby. There is a risk from taking the medicine and a risk should you stop a medicine, e.g. you might become ill again and need to go back on the medication. The advice offered here is just that—**advice**, but may give you some idea about the possible risks and what (at the time of writing) is known through the medical press.

It may be helpful to know that in the USA, the FDA (Federal Drug Administration) classifies medicines in pregnancy in five groups:

A =	Studies show no risk, so harm to the unborn child appears only a remote possibility
B =	Animal and human studies indicate a lack of risk, but are not fully conclusive
C =	Animal studies indicate a risk, but there is no safety date in humans
D =	A definite risk exists, but the benefit may outweigh the risk in some people
X =	The risk outweighs any possible benefit

Valproate is classified as 'D'. There is some evidence of problems, e.g. a 1 in 100 chance of spina bifida and a 'valproate syndrome'. You will need to seek personal advice from an expert, as counselling and screening at a specialist centre is recommended. Taking folic acid supplements before becoming pregnant and throughout pregnancy may reduce this risk. You will, of course, also need to consider the risk of relapse if you stop your valproate. One study suggested that there might be a slightly higher chance of a child having higher educational needs if the mother took valproate throughout pregnancy, but this has not been proven yet. If you are taking valproate for epilepsy, then you will also need to consider the risk of seizures, if the medication is stopped.

Will I need blood tests?

For the first six months of treatment you will need a regular blood test (e.g. every month) to check that the drug is not affecting your liver.

You may then need to have blood tests from time to time to ensure that the dose of valproate is enough and not too much or too little to control the condition for which it has been prescribed.

Can I drive while taking valproate?

If you have epilepsy, it is essential that you report this, as well as sudden disabling attacks of loss or partial loss of consciousness, to the 'Driver and Vehicle Licensing Centre' (DVLC). The DVLC will then make a medical assessment of your condition, consulting with your doctor(s) where necessary. For more information see leaflet 'D100' (*'What you need to know about driving licensing'*), which is available from most post offices, or contact the Driver Enquiry Unit, DVLC, SWANSEA SA6 7JL. (Telephone: 01792 772134 between 8.15am. and 4.30pm. Monday to Friday). You will need to quote your driver number whether you write or telephone. Alternatively, visit the DVLA website, page:

www.dvla.gov.uk/at_a_glance/content.htm.

If you are allowed to drive, remember that valproate can make you drowsy when you first start taking it, so extra care should be taken when driving or operating any type of machinery.

It is advisable to let your insurance company know if you are taking this drug. If you do not and you have an accident, it could affect your insurance cover.

If you are advised by your doctor not to drive, and continue to do so, the General Medical Council has advised doctors to inform the DVLA. The DVLA may then carry out an enquiry.

Treatments for problems with mood

Drugs known as mood stabilisers (sometimes known as antimanics and mood normalisers)

Drug: Lithium

Drugs available	Brand name(s)	Forms available			
		Tablets	Capsules	Liquid	Injection
Lithium carbonate	Camcolit®	✔			
	Liskonum®	✔			
	Priadel®	✔			
Lithium citrate	Litarex®	✔			
	Priadel®			✔ (sugar-free)	
	Li-liquid®			✔ (sugar-free)	

For what is lithium used?

Lithium is mainly used to help to normalise or even out mood swings. It can help if you are either low or high. It can also help to prevent future mood swings in people who suffer from manic depression, also known as bipolar mood disorder or bipolar affective disorder. It is one of a number of drugs that can help to stabilise moods. Lithium is also used to help treat many other conditions, e.g. aggression.

How does lithium work?

It is not known exactly how lithium works. There are many theories, but it probably evens out or stabilises the speed at which the brain passes messages, and stabilises cells, nerves, and 'secondary messengers'. Lithium itself is chemically similar to the sodium in salt.

How should I take it?

Tablets:

Tablets should be swallowed with at least half a glass of water while sitting or standing, so that they reach the stomach and do not stick in the throat. 'Litarex®', 'Liskonum®', 'Camcolit 400®', and 'Priadel®' tablets should be swallowed whole and not chewed. These tablets are made so that they release the lithium over a longer period of time. This can help to reduce side-effects, or reduce the number of times a day you need to take the medication. If you cannot swallow these whole, they can be broken. Do not crush, chew, or dissolve the tablets, as this will cause the drug to be released too quickly and you may experience more side-effects.

Liquids:

Your pharmacist should give you a medicine spoon or an oral syringe (ask for a medicine spoon if you do not have one). Use it carefully to measure the correct amount.

When should I take it?

Take the doses as directed on the medicine label. You should take it at regular times or a regular time each day. Taking a dose at mealtimes may make it easier to remember, and there is no problem about taking lithium with or after food. If the instructions say to take lithium **once** a day, this is usually better taken at bedtime. You should avoid sudden changes in dose.

How long will lithium take to work?

It may take several weeks before you begin to improve. For people who suffer from manic depression, it may take many months before the depressive part of this illness improves.

For how long will I need to keep taking lithium?

You should talk about this with your doctor as people's responses are different. Lithium usually needs to be taken for some time. As well as treating the illness, lithium also helps to prevent the symptoms returning. Once you have started lithium, you may need to take it for a long time, at least two or three years, and quite possibly much longer. For it to continue working, lithium must be taken every day.

Is lithium addictive?

Lithium is not addictive as such, but many people experience some effects if medication is stopped suddenly (see below).

Can I stop taking lithium suddenly?

Absolutely not. It is very unwise to stop taking lithium suddenly, even if you feel better. Many recent studies have shown that if you stop lithium suddenly (i.e. over 1–14 days) you have a one in two (50%) chance of becoming ill again within six months and a 90% chance of becoming ill again within four years. If you need to stop lithium, it should be done gradually over at least four weeks, preferably longer, i.e. 3–6 months. The dose should be decreased **gradually** during this time to minimise possible problems. (See also '*For how long will I need to keep taking lithium?*' above)

What should I do if I forget to take a dose?

Start again as soon as you remember unless it is almost time for your next dose, then go on as before. Do not try to catch up by taking two or more doses at once, as you may experience more side-effects. You should tell your doctor about this at your next appointment. If you miss several doses start again when you remember and tell your doctor. You may need a new blood test to check that there is enough, but not too much, lithium in your blood. If you miss an occasional dose (e.g. a day, or two every few weeks) it is unlikely that you will become ill again.

If you have problems remembering your doses (as many people do) ask your pharmacist, doctor, or nurse about this. There are special packs, boxes, and devices available that can be used to help you remember.

Will lithium make me drowsy?

Lithium may make you feel drowsy at first. You should not drive (see below) or operate machinery until you know how it affects you. You should take extra care, as this may affect your reflexes or reaction times.

Will lithium cause weight gain?

It is not uncommon for people to put on some weight when taking lithium. This may, in part, be caused by a common side-effect of lithium therapy—feeling thirsty, and drinking large amounts of high calorie drinks can encourage weight gain. If this happens, try drinks that are low in calories, e.g. low calorie squash or water, and cut down on sugar and milk in your tea and coffee. It is impossible to know what the effect on your weight will be because each person's responses are different. It is important that you do not ignore feelings of thirst, as this can lead to lithium poisoning. This is very important, especially if you go on holiday to a hot country where you may sweat heavily (see side-effects above).

If your weight does increase or you have other problems, your doctor can arrange for you to see a dietician for advice. Any weight you put on can be controlled while you are still taking this medication, with expert advice about diet. In some people weight gain can be a serious problem. If it causes you distress, discuss with your doctor at your next appointment. A change in your dose may be necessary in extreme cases.

Will lithium affect my sex life?

Drugs can affect desire (libido), arousal (erection), and orgasmic ability. Lithium has not been reported to have a major adverse effect on these three stages. However, if this does seem to happen, you should discuss this with your doctor, as a change in dose may help minimise problems.

Can I drink alcohol while I am taking lithium?

There is no complete ban on drinking alcohol if you are taking lithium, but limit yourself to one or two drinks a day, as this may affect the level of lithium in your blood. It may also cause you to feel drowsier. This is especially important if you need to drive or operate machinery, as it can affect reaction times. You should seek advice on this.

Are there any foods or drinks that I should avoid?

It is important that you do not drink too much or too little fluid, (e.g. do not ignore feelings of thirst) as this can lead to lithium poisoning. However, drinking high calorie drinks can cause you to put on weight (see weight gain above). Drinks containing caffeine, e.g. coffee, tea, or cola, can cause an increased lithium effect, so take some decaffeinated drinks as well.

Do not have a low salt diet. Lithium is closely related to sodium salts in the body and this can lead to lithium poisoning.

Will lithium affect my other medication?

There are a number of drugs that can affect the lithium levels in your blood. You should tell your doctor before stopping or starting any other medication. You should also show your lithium card to any doctor, dentist, or pharmacist who may treat you. If you need a pain killer or analgesic, you should take paracetamol rather than aspirin or ibuprofen ('Nurofen®' etc). If taken regularly, ibuprofen can cause the lithium level in your blood to rise and that can lead to lithium poisoning and occasionally aspirin can have the same effects. Other drugs that can interact with lithium include: treatments for high blood pressure (e.g. diuretics), arthritis, asthma, and infections. This does not necessarily mean the drugs cannot be used together, just that you may need to follow your doctor's instructions very carefully.

If I am taking a contraceptive pill, will this be affected?

It is not thought that the contraceptive pill is affected by lithium.

What if I want to start a family or discover I'm pregnant?

It is important to consider that there will be a risk to you and your child from taking a medicine during pregnancy, but also a possible risk from stopping the medicine, e.g. suffering a relapse. Unfortunately, no decision is risk-free. It will be for you to decide which is the least risk. All we can do here is to help you understand some of the issues, so you can make an informed decision. For your information, major malformations occur 'spontaneously' in about 2–4% of all pregnancies, even if no drugs are taken. The main problem with medicines is termed 'teratogenicity', i.e. a medicine causing a malformation in the unborn child. A medicine causing teratogenicity is called a 'teratogen'. Since a baby has completed its main development between days 17 and 60 of the pregnancy (the so-called 'first trimester'), these first 2–16 weeks are the main concern. After that, there may be other problems, e.g. some medicines may cause slower growth. The infant may also be affected after birth, e.g. withdrawal effects are possible with some drugs.

If possible, the best option is to plan in advance. If you think you could become pregnant, discuss this with your doctor and it may be possible to switch to medicines thought to carry least risk, and take other risk-reducing steps, e.g. adjusting doses, taking vitamin supplements, etc. If you have just discovered you are pregnant, don't panic, but, if possible, seek advice from your GP within the next few days. He or she may also want to refer you on to someone with more specialist knowledge of your medicine.

Very few medicines have been shown to be completely safe in pregnancy, so no manufacturer or advisor can ever say any medicine is safe. They will usually advise not to take a medicine during pregnancy, unless the benefit is much greater than the risk. In the UK, there is the NTIS (National Teratology Information Service) which offers individual risk assessments. However, its advice should always be used to help you and your doctor decide what is the risk to you and your baby. There is a risk from taking the medicine and a risk should you stop a medicine, e.g. you might become ill again and need to go back on the medication. The advice offered here is just that—**advice**, but may give you some idea about the possible risks and what (at the time of writing) is known through the medical press.

It may be helpful to know that in the USA, the FDA (Federal Drug Administration) classifies medicines in pregnancy in five groups:

A =	Studies show no risk, so harm to the unborn child appears only a remote possibility
B =	Animal and human studies indicate a lack of risk, but are not fully conclusive
C =	Animal studies indicate a risk, but there is no safety date in humans
D =	A definite risk exists, but the benefit may outweigh the risk in some people
X =	The risk outweighs any possible benefit

Lithium is classified as 'D'. There is much controversy about lithium in pregnancy. Early data from Scandinavia indicated a problem, but recent studies have indicated that the risk of problems is only slightly higher than in women not taking lithium. The other things to consider are that:

- if you have become pregnant unexpectedly, the risk of relapsing over the next six months if you stop lithium suddenly is very high (as high as 50%)

- by the time you realise you are pregnant, the potential effect would already have happened, so stopping suddenly would be too late anyway.

The major risk with lithium in pregnancy is something called Ebstein's anomaly, a rare heart defect in the child. The chance of this happening without lithium is about 1 in 20,000 children, and this rises to about 1 in 1000 with lithium (i.e. 20 times higher, but still rare). This heart problem can be detected, so you should seek personal advice from your GP, who will arrange for specialist screening to be carried out. Regular blood monitoring will be important as you get closer to your due date, as lithium levels may rise towards the end of pregnancy. One piece of good news is that one study was able to show that, if the mum took lithium throughout pregnancy, lithium did not appear to have an effect on physical or mental development over the first 5–10 years of the child's life.

What sort of side-effects might occur?

Side-effect	What happens	What to do about it
Common		
Tremor	Fine shaking of the hands	This is not dangerous, but can be irritating. If it annoys you, your doctor may be able to give you something for it (e.g. propranolol). If it worsens and spreads to the legs or jaw, stop taking the lithium and see your doctor
Stomach upset	This includes feeling and being sick, and having diarrhoea	If it is mild, see your pharmacist. If it lasts for more than a day, see your doctor
Polyuria	Passing excessive amounts of urine	Do not drink too much alcohol. Tell your doctor about it. Some blood and urine tests may be needed
Metallic taste	Your mouth tastes as if has had metal or something bitter in it	This should wear off after a few weeks. If it does not, mention it to your doctor at your next appointment. A change in dose may help
Polydipsia	Feeling very thirsty. Your mouth is dry and there may be a metallic taste	Drink water or low calorie drinks in moderation. Suck sugar-free boiled sweets
Less common		
Weight gain	Eating and drinking more, and putting on weight	A diet high in vegetables and fibre may help prevent weight gain. See also a separate question in this section. Seek help from a dietician
Hypothyroidism	Low thyroid activity— this makes you feel tired	This is not serious. Tell your doctor at your next appointment. It may be necessary to take some thyroid replacement
Rare		
Skin rashes	Blotches seen anywhere	Stop taking and see your doctor
Blurred vision	Things look fuzzy and you cannot focus properly	Your lithium level may be too high. Stop taking and contact your doctor now
Drowsiness	Feeling sleepy and sluggish in the daytime	
Confusion	Your mind is all mixed up	
Palpitations	A fast heart beat	

Table adapted from UK Psychiatric Pharmacy Group leaflets, with kind permission (www.ukppg.org.uk)

Do not worry about this list of side-effects, as you may not experience any. There are other rare side-effects. If you develop any unusual symptoms, ask your doctor about these at your next appointment.

The following side-effects may show that the level of lithium in your blood is too high:

- blurred vision
- diarrhoea and vomiting
- unsteadiness
- difficulty in speaking
- severe tremor
- clumsiness
- very much increased thirst or passing excessive urine
- severe drowsiness, confusion, or sluggishness.

If you experience any of these side-effects, do not take any more tablets and contact your doctor as soon as possible, within the next day or two.

You should avoid exercise in hot weather, or other activities that cause heavy sweating (e.g. a sauna). If your dose and blood is monitored well, lithium does not have any major long-term side-effects.

Will I need a blood test ?

The aim of treatment is for the lithium in your blood to reach the level needed to help your symptoms, but not to reach a level high enough to cause side-effects. Each person is different and so your lithium dose needs to be exact for you. It will depend on your age, weight, height, etc. To control this, a blood sample needs to be taken and checked. This will need to be done every week at the start of treatment, but can be reduced later to every three months. When you are stable, make sure that you have a blood test at least every three months. You may need to have extra tests if you experience any increase in side-effects (see previous pages for a list of these). If you have diarrhoea (the 'runs'), if you have to take any drugs that might interact with the lithium, or if the weather is very hot; all these things can upset your lithium level and cause side-effects.

If you normally have a dose in the morning and a blood test within four hours, you should delay this morning dose until after your blood test or it will upset the result.

Can I drive while I am taking lithium?

You may feel drowsy and/or confused when first taking lithium. Until this wears off or you know how your drug affects you, do not drive or operate any type of machinery. You should take extra care, as this may affect your reaction times or reflexes.

It is an offence to drive, to attempt to drive, or to be in charge of a vehicle when unfit through drugs. It is advisable to let your insurance company know if you are taking lithium. If you do not and you have an accident, it could affect your insurance cover.

If you are advised by your doctor not to drive, and continue to do so, the General Medical Council has advised doctors to inform the DVLA. The DVLA may then carry out an enquiry.

Additional information

Your pharmacist or doctor should give you a lithium card when you collect your first course of lithium unless you are on a very low dose. You should carry this with you at all times. Show the card to your doctor and pharmacist each time you receive a new supply. You should also show it to any doctor, dentist, or pharmacist who may treat you. If you lose the card, ask for a new one. Your pharmacist should be able to give you one.

Treatments for lack of sleep (insomnia)

Drugs known as hypnotics or 'sleeping tablets'

Drug group: Benzodiazepines

Drugs available	Brand name(s)	Forms available			
		Tablets	Capsules	Liquid	Injection
*Flunitrazepam	Rohypnol®	✔			
*Flurazepam	Dalmane®		✔		
Loprazolam		✔			
Lormetazepam		✔			
Nitrazepam	Many [1]	✔		✔	
Temazepam		✔		✔	

*   These products are not available on the NHS
1. Nitrazepam is available as Remnos®, and Somnite®, as well as the better-known Mogadon®.

What are they used for?

Hypnotics make you sleepy and are used as a short-term treatment of insomnia (difficulty in falling or staying asleep). The benzodiazepines are also 'calmers'. They help to calm you down and can make you sleepy, particularly if you are also anxious. As well as making sure the causes of your insomnia are treated, you should ensure that you have good 'sleep hygiene'. Your bed should be comfortable, you should sleep in a quiet room, drink no caffeine within two hours of going to bed, and keep regular habits, e.g. a bedtime routine, possibly with a warm, milky drink before going to bed.

How do they work?

Hypnotics reduce the alertness of the brain and this helps you to sleep. GABA is a chemical messenger (or 'neurotransmitter') and is the brain's own naturally occurring 'calmer'. The benzodiazepines enhance the action of GABA, making it more powerful, and this calms the brain and helps you to fall asleep.

How should I take them?

Tablets and capsules:

Tablets and capsules should be swallowed with at least half a glass of water while sitting or standing. This is to ensure that they reach the stomach and do not stick in the throat.

Liquids:

Your pharmacist should give you a medicine spoon. Use it carefully to measure the correct amount. Ask your pharmacist for a medicine spoon if you do not have one.

Shake the bottle well before use, as the drug can settle to the bottom. This could result in you receiving too low a dose at the start and too high a dose at the end of the bottle.

When should I take them?

Take your medication at bedtime, as directed on the medicine label. Take them about half an hour before you want to go to sleep. Do not take a further dose if you wake up later unless specifically told to do so.

How long will they take to work?

They should start to work about half an hour after you take them. If they do not or make you too sleepy the next morning, your doctor may need to adjust the dose to suit you.

For how long will I need to keep taking them?

This should be discussed with your doctor, as each person's response is different. Benzodiazepines are very safe drugs if used sensibly. They are best taken in as low a dose as possible for a short time, e.g. as a 'first aid' measure. Usually, this should be for no longer than about one month to help you overcome your problems, and for other treatments to start working. If you need to take them for longer, you should discuss this regularly with your doctor. Some people with long-term problems may need to take them for longer.

Are they addictive?

Due to the effects that benzodiazepines have on the brain, they can cause dependence or addiction in some people if taken regularly every day for more than about four to six weeks. This is unlikely if you are only taking them as sleeping tablets, but it can still happen. It is better to take them only when you need them.

Can I stop taking them suddenly?

If you have been taking them every day for more than four to six weeks and you stop them suddenly, this may cause a few problems. It is possible that for a few nights you may not sleep very well (this is called 'rebound insomnia'). Generally, this does not last long, e.g. for more than a couple of days. If you have any problems discuss these with your doctor, as it may be possible to start again and then reduce your dose slowly.

What should I do if I forget to take them?

Take the dose as soon as you remember. If you take it too late at night you may feel drowsier the next morning. If you managed to fall asleep without them, try missing the dose again the next night.

Will they make me drowsy?

Hypnotics are used to help you sleep and should make you feel drowsy. You may, however, feel drowsy the next morning, so you should not drive (see below) or operate machinery until you know how they affect you. You should take extra care as they may affect your reaction times, even if you feel well.

Will they cause weight gain?

It is not thought that the benzodiazepines cause changes in weight. However, if you do start to have problems, tell your doctor at your next appointment and he/she can arrange for you to see a dietician for advice.

Will it affect my sex life?

Benzodiazepine hypnotics do not have any known significant effects, unless of course you are too sleepy or have already gone to sleep.

What sort of side-effects might occur?

Side-effect	What happens	What to do about it
Common		
Drowsiness	You feel sleepy or sluggish the next morning	Do not drive or use machinery. Discuss with your doctor—it may be better to adjust the dose, or try a different drug
Dizziness	Feeling light-headed and faint	Do not stand up too quickly. Try and lie or sit down if you feel it coming on. Do not drive or operate machinery
Less common		
Ataxia	Being unsteady on your feet	Discuss with your doctor at your next appointment. It may be best to adjust your drug or dose
Rare		
Aggression	Feeling excitable. You may be talkative, unfriendly, or disinhibited	Discuss this with your doctor. He/she may want to adjust your drug or dose
Headache	Your head is pounding and painful	Try aspirin or paracetamol. Your pharmacist will be able to advise if these are safe to take with other drugs you may be taking
Confusion	Your mind is all mixed up or confused	Discuss with your doctor at your next appointment. He/she may want to adjust your drug or dose
Hypotension	Low blood pressure— this can make you feel dizzy, particularly when you stand up	It is not dangerous. Do not stand up too quickly. If you feel dizzy, do not drive
Amnesia	Loss of short-term memory or difficulty in remembering	It is not dangerous. Discuss with your doctor if you are worried
Rashes	Blotches seen anywhere	Stop taking the drug and see your doctor now

Table adapted from UK Psychiatric Pharmacy Group leaflets, with kind permission (www.ukppg.org.uk)

Do not worry about this list of side-effects, as you may not experience any. There are other rare side-effects. If you develop any unusual symptoms, ask your doctor about these at your next appointment.

Can I drink alcohol while I am taking these?

If you drink alcohol while taking these drugs, they may make you feel sleepier. This is particularly important if you need to drive or operate machinery, and you must seek advice on this. They may affect your reflexes or reaction times. They can also increase the effects of alcohol, so it is better to avoid alcohol. If you take alcohol the next day, e.g. at lunchtime, this can also make you feel drowsier than you would expect.

Are there any foods or drinks that I should avoid?

You should have no problems with any food or drink other than alcohol (see above).

Will they affect my other medication?

Generally, you should not have problems with other medications, although some have occurred. Make sure your doctor knows about all the medicines you are taking. The benzodiazepines can 'interact' with other sleeping drugs and some antidepressants by increasing their sedative effect, although your doctor should know about these. Some other medicines, e.g. the painkiller, co-proxamol ('Distalgesic'®) can make you drowsy. When combined with your benzodiazepine, this could make you even drowsier. This does not necessarily mean the drugs cannot be used together, just that you may need to follow your doctor's instructions very carefully. You should tell your doctor before starting or stopping these or any other drugs.

If I am taking a contraceptive pill, will this be affected?

It is not thought that the contraceptive pill is affected by any of these drugs.

What if I want to start a family or discover I'm pregnant?

It is important to consider that there will be a risk to you and your child from taking a medicine during pregnancy, but also a possible risk from stopping the medicine, e.g. suffering a relapse. Unfortunately, no decision is risk-free. It will be for you to decide which is the least risk. All we can do here is to help you understand some of the issues, so you can make an informed decision. For your information, major malformations occur 'spontaneously' in about 2–4% of all pregnancies, even if no drugs are taken. The main problem with medicines is termed 'teratogenicity', i.e. a medicine causing a malformation in the unborn child. A medicine causing teratogenicity is called a 'teratogen'. Since a baby has completed its main development between days 17 and 60 of the pregnancy (the so-called 'first trimester'), these first 2–16 weeks are the main concern. After that, there may be other problems, e.g. some medicines may cause slower growth. The infant may also be affected after birth, e.g. withdrawal effects are possible with some drugs.

If possible, the best option is to plan in advance. If you think you could become pregnant, discuss this with your doctor and it may be possible to switch to medicines thought to carry least risk, and take other risk-reducing steps, e.g. adjusting doses, taking vitamin supplements, etc. If you have just discovered you are pregnant, don't panic, but, if possible, seek advice from your GP within the next few days. He or she may also want to refer you on to someone with more specialist knowledge of your medicine.

Very few medicines have been shown to be completely safe in pregnancy, so no manufacturer or advisor can ever say any medicine is safe. They will usually advise not to take a medicine during pregnancy, unless the benefit is much greater than the risk. In the UK, there is the NTIS (National Teratology Information Service) which offers individual risk assessments. However, its advice should always be used to help you and your doctor decide what is the risk to you and your baby. There is a risk from taking the medicine and a risk should you stop a medicine, e.g. you might become ill again and need to go back on the medication. The advice offered here is just that—**advice**, but may give you some idea about the possible risks and what (at the time of writing) is known through the medical press.

It may be helpful to know that in the USA, the FDA (Federal Drug Administration) classifies medicines in pregnancy in five groups:

A =	Studies show no risk, so harm to the unborn child appears only a remote possibility
B =	Animal and human studies indicate a lack of risk, but are not fully conclusive
C =	Animal studies indicate a risk, but there is no safety date in humans
D =	A definite risk exists, but the benefit may outweigh the risk in some people
X =	The risk outweighs any possible benefit

Temazepam is classified as 'X'. The others are not classified. Although some studies have shown a slightly increased chance of abnormalities with benzodiazepines, alcohol and other drug use may have been the reason for this. The risk of oral clefts is reported to be about 1 in 150 births of children born to mothers who took diazepam throughout pregnancy. Occasional use of shorter-acting benzodiazepines would appear to have a very low risk. Regular use of longer-acting benzodiazepines (e.g. chlordiazepoxide, diazepam) may also lead to some short-term breathing difficulties in newborn babies, and some withdrawal effects, e.g. the floppy baby syndrome. You should seek personal advice from your GP, who may then, if necessary, seek further specialist advice.

Will I need a blood test?

You will not need to have a blood test to check on your benzodiazepine.

Can I drive while I am taking them?

The benzodiazepines can reduce your ability to carry out skilled tasks, such as driving or operating machinery. You may also feel drowsy the day after you take them. Until these effects wear off or you know how your drug affects you, do not drive or operate machinery. You should take extra care, as they may affect your reaction times.

It is an offence to drive, to attempt to drive, or to be in charge of a vehicle when unfit through drugs. This would include sleeping tablets. It is advisable to let your insurance company know if you are taking these drugs. If you do not and you have an accident, it could affect your insurance cover.

If you are advised by your doctor not to drive, and continue to do so, the General Medical Council has advised doctors to inform the DVLA. The DVLA may then carry out an enquiry.

Drug group: Non-benzodiazepines

Drugs available	Brand name(s)	Forms available			
		Tablets	**Capsules**	**Liquid**	**Injection**
Chloral hydrate				✔	
Chloral betaine	Welldorm®	✔		✔	
Clomethiazole or chlormethiazole	Heminevrin®		✔	✔ (sugar-free)	
Diphenhydramine	Nytol® Medinex®	✔		✔	
Promethazine	Phenergan® Sominex® Q-Mazine®	✔		✔	✔
Zaleplon	Sonata®		✔		
Zolpidem	Stilnoct®	✔			
Zopiclone	Zimovane®	✔			

Chlormethiazole has changed its name to clomethiazole, although both are still in use.

For what are they used?

Hypnotics make you sleepy and are used as a short-term treatment for insomnia (difficulty in falling or staying asleep). Clomethiazole ('Heminevrin®') can also be used to help agitation and restlessness, and to help alcohol withdrawal symptoms.

How do they work?

Hypnotics make you sleepy and are used as a short-term treatment for insomnia (difficulty in falling or staying asleep). They help to calm you down and can make you sleepy, particularly if you are also anxious.

As well as making sure that the causes of your insomnia are treated, you should ensure good 'sleep hygiene'. You should sleep in a comfortable bed, in a quiet room, drink no caffeine within two hours of going to bed, and ensure regular habits, e.g. a bedtime routine, possibly with a warm, milky drink before going to bed.

How should I take them?

Tablets and capsules:

Tablets and capsules should be swallowed with at least half a glass of water while sitting or standing. This is to ensure that they reach the stomach and do not stick in the throat. It is especially important that you take chloral with plenty of water or milk to avoid upsetting your stomach.

Liquids:

Your pharmacist should give you a medicine spoon. Use it carefully to measure the correct amount. Ask your pharmacist for a medicine spoon if you do not have one. You should take chloral hydrate with plenty of water or milk to avoid upsetting your stomach. Chloral hydrate syrup and chlormethiazole/clomethiazole syrup ('Heminevrin®') do not taste very nice. You could add fruit juices or squash just before taking them if you want to make them more palatable.

When should I take them?

Take your medication at bedtime as directed on the medicine label. Take it about half an hour to an hour before you want to go to sleep. Do not take another dose if you wake up later unless specifically told to do so. You can take zaleplon or zolpidem when going to bed, or delay and use it only if you cannot sleep. Either way, be prepared to go to sleep for at least three to four hours within 15–60 minutes of taking your dose.

How long will they take to work?

They should start to work about half an hour to an hour after you take them. If they do not or make you too sleepy the next morning, your doctor may need to adjust the drug or dose to suit you.

For how long will I need to keep taking them?

This should be discussed with your doctor as people's responses are different. They are safe drugs if used sensibly. They should be taken in as low a dose as possible for the shortest possible time. Ideally, this is for no longer than one month to help overcome your problems. If you need to take them for longer, you should discuss this regularly with your doctor. Taking them only when required or every few days (e.g. alternate nights) can be a useful way to use these drugs safely.

It is not recommended that chlormethiazole/clomethiazole is taken for longer than nine days if used to help alcohol withdrawal.

Are they addictive?

Due to the effects that these drugs have on the brain, they can sometimes produce a type of dependence (or addiction) in some people if taken regularly every night for more than four to six weeks. Dependence or addiction means that you cannot manage without them because if you stop taking them, you experience 'withdrawal' symptoms. These withdrawal symptoms could, at worst, include: anxiety, tension, poor concentration, difficulty in sleeping, i.e. 'rebound insomnia', palpitations, and sweating. This is unlikely at normal doses. These withdrawal symptoms may occur several days after stopping your drug. They may last for a few weeks, but could go on for longer. If you have taken them for a long period of time, your doctor may need to take you off your hypnotic by gradually reducing your dose over a period of time to prevent these effects. It is also true that many people suffer no withdrawal symptoms at all when they stop, even if they have been taking hypnotics for a while. Thus, you should make sure that you discuss your particular treatment with your doctor.

If someone has a drink problem and is taking clomethiazole to help the withdrawal symptoms, it is inadvisable to take the drug for more than nine days, as he/she may become addicted to clomethiazole instead of alcohol.

Can I stop taking them suddenly?

It is probably better not to stop chloral, clomethiazole and zopiclone suddenly if you have been taking more than one dose regularly every day for over four weeks. If you do, you may suffer some of the withdrawal effects mentioned above. If you take them only when really necessary, this is better than taking them continuously and may prevent you from becoming dependent on them. You should discuss this with your doctor.

What should I do if I forget to take them?

Take the dose as soon as you remember. If you take it too late at night, you may feel drowsier the next morning.

What sort of side-effects might occur?

Side-effect	What happens	What to do about it
Zopiclone		
Drowsiness, or dizziness	You feel sleepy or sluggish the next morning	Do not drive or use machinery. Discuss with your doctor—it may be better to adjust the dose or try a different drug
Bitter or metallic taste	Your mouth tastes as if has had metal or something bitter in it	This should wear off after a few weeks. If it does not, mention it to your doctor at your next appointment. A change in dose or drug may help
Headache	Your head is pounding and painful	Try aspirin or paracetamol. Your pharmacist will be able to advise if these are safe to take with other drugs you may be taking
Stomach upset	This includes feeling sick (nausea) and diarrhoea (the runs)	If you feel like this for more than a week after starting the zopiclone, tell your doctor
Changes in behaviour	Feeling excitable. You may be talkative, unfriendly, disinhibited, or irritable	Discuss this with your doctor. He/she may want to adjust your drug or dose
Zolpidem		
Drowsiness, or dizziness	You feel sleepy or sluggish the next morning	Do not drive or use machinery. Discuss with your doctor—it may be better to adjust the dose or try a different drug
Headache	Your head is pounding and painful	Try aspirin or paracetamol. Your pharmacist will be able to advise if these are safe to take with other drugs you may be taking
Stomach upset	This includes feeling sick (nausea) and diarrhoea (the runs)	If you feel like this for more than a week after starting the zolpidem, tell your doctor
Changes in behaviour	Feeling excitable. You may be talkative, unfriendly, or disinhibited	Discuss this with your doctor. He/she may want to adjust your drug or dose
Amnesia	Loss of short-term memory or difficulty in remembering	It is not dangerous. Discuss with your doctor if you are worried
Zaleplon		
Headache	Your head is pounding and painful	Try aspirin or paracetamol. Your pharmacist will be able to advise if these are safe to take with the other drugs you may be taking
Drowsiness or dizziness	You feel sleepy or sluggish the next morning	Do not drive or use machinery. Discuss with your doctor—it may be better to adjust the dose or try a different drug
Amnesia	Loss of short-term memory or difficulty in remembering	It is not dangerous. Discuss with your doctor if you are worried
Chloral		
Stomach upset	Feeling sick, stomach pains, and diarrhoea (the runs)	If you feel like this for more than a week after starting the chloral, tell your doctor
Drowsiness or dizziness	You feel sleepy or sluggish the next morning	Do not drive or use machinery. Discuss with your doctor—it may be better to adjust the dose or try a different drug
Headache	Your head is pounding and painful	Try aspirin or paracetamol. Your pharmacist will be able to advise if these are safe to take with other drugs you may be taking
Rashes	Blotches seen anywhere	Stop taking the drug and see your doctor now
Confusion or hallucinations	Your mind is all mixed up, confused, or you begin imagining things	Discuss with your doctor at your next appointment. He/she may want to adjust your drug or dose

Side-effect	What happens	What to do about it
Wheeziness	Difficulty in breathing and your chest feels tight. This may happen if you have asthma	Contact your doctor now
Chlormethiazole/clomethiazole		
Drowsiness or dizziness	You feel sleepy or sluggish the next morning	Do not drive or use machinery. Discuss with your doctor—it may be better to adjust the dose or try a different drug
Nasal congestion and sneezing	This may occur 15 to 20 minutes after taking this drug	This should wear off after a while, but if it does not or causes you discomfort, you should discuss this with your doctor
Antihistamines (Diphenhydramine and promethazine)		
Drowsiness	You feel sleepy or sluggish the next morning	Do not drive or use machinery. Discuss with your doctor—it may be better to adjust the dose or try a different drug
Dizziness	Feeling light-headed and faint	Do not stand up too quickly. Try and lie or sit down if you feel it coming on. Do not drive
Headache	Your head is pounding and painful	Try aspirin or paracetamol. Your pharmacist will be able to advise if these are safe to take with other drugs you may be taking
Anticholinergic side-effects	Dry mouth, blurred vision, difficulty in passing urine, or constipation	These are usually mild and should wear off after a few weeks. If not, contact your doctor or pharmacist
Photosensitivity	Becoming blotchy in the sun	This is uncommon. If it occurs, avoid direct sunlight or sun lamps. Use a high factor sun block cream
Wheeziness	Difficulty in breathing and feelings of tightness in the chest. This may happen if you have asthma	Stop taking the drug and contact your doctor
Palpitations	A fast heart beat	It is rare, but if it happens stop taking the drug and contact your doctor to discuss it

Table adapted from UK Psychiatric Pharmacy Group leaflets, with kind permission (www.ukppg.org.uk)

Do not worry about this list of side-effects, as you may not experience any. There are other rare side-effects. If you develop any unusual symptoms ask your doctor about these at your next appointment.

Will they make me drowsy?

Hypnotics are used to help you sleep and should make you feel drowsy. You may, however, feel drowsy the next morning, so you should not drive or operate machinery until you know how they affect you. You should take extra care, as they may affect your reaction times, even if you feel well.

Will they cause weight gain?

It is not thought that any of these hypnotics cause changes in weight. If you do start to have problems, tell your doctor at your next appointment and he/she can arrange an appointment with a dietician for advice.

Will it affect my sex life?

These hypnotics do not have any known significant effects, unless of course you are too sleepy or have already gone to sleep.

Can I drink alcohol while I am taking these drugs?

You should avoid alcohol while taking these drugs as they may make you feel sleepier. This is particularly important if you need to drive or operate machinery, and you must seek advice on this. The hypnotics can also increase the effects of alcohol. If you take alcohol the next day, e.g. lunchtime, this can also make you feel drowsier than you would expect.

Are there any foods or drinks that I should avoid?

You should have no problems with any food or drink other than alcohol (see above).

Will they affect my other medication?

Problems with other medications are uncommon, although a few have been recorded. Chloral can 'interact' with some anticoagulants, and clomethiazole can 'interact' with cimetidine ('Tagamet®', a treatment for stomach ulcers). They can also interact with other sleeping drugs and some antidepressants by increasing their sedative effects. This does not necessarily mean the drugs cannot be used together, just that you may need to follow your doctor's instructions very carefully. Make sure your doctor knows about all the medicines you are taking. Some other medicines, e.g. the painkiller co-proxamol ('Distalgesic®') and some antihistamines (for hay fever) can make you drowsy. When combined with your hypnotic, this could make you even drowsier. You should tell your doctor before starting or stopping these, or any other drugs and ask your pharmacist before buying medicine over the counter.

If I am taking a contraceptive pill, will this be affected?

It is not thought that the contraceptive pill is affected by any of these drugs.

What if I want to start a family or discover I'm pregnant?

It is important to consider that there will be a risk to you and your child from taking a medicine during pregnancy, but also a possible risk from stopping the medicine, e.g. suffering a relapse. Unfortunately, no decision is risk-free. It will be for you to decide which is the least risk. All we can do here is to help you understand some of the issues, so you can make an informed decision. For your information, major malformations occur 'spontaneously' in about 2–4% of all pregnancies, even if no drugs are taken. The main problem with medicines is termed 'teratogenicity', i.e. a medicine causing a malformation in the unborn child. A medicine causing teratogenicity is called a 'teratogen'. Since a baby has completed its main development between days 17 and 60 of the pregnancy (the so-called 'first trimester'), these first 2–16 weeks are the main concern. After that, there may be other problems, e.g. some medicines may cause slower growth. The infant may also be affected after birth, e.g. withdrawal effects are possible with some drugs.

If possible, the best option is to plan in advance. If you think you could become pregnant, discuss this with your doctor and it may be possible to switch to medicines thought to carry least risk, and take other risk-reducing steps, e.g. adjusting doses, taking vitamin supplements, etc. If you have just discovered you are pregnant, don't panic, but, if possible, seek advice from your GP within the next few days. He or she may also want to refer you on to someone with more specialist knowledge of your medicine.

Very few medicines have been shown to be completely safe in pregnancy, so no manufacturer or advisor can ever say any medicine is safe. They will usually advise not to take a medicine during pregnancy, unless the benefit is much greater than the risk. In the UK, there is the NTIS (National Teratology

Information Service) which offers individual risk assessments. However, its advice should always be used to help you and your doctor decide what is the risk to you and your baby. There is a risk from taking the medicine and a risk should you stop a medicine, e.g. you might become ill again and need to go back on the medication. The advice offered here is just that—**advice**, but may give you some idea about the possible risks and what (at the time of writing) is known through the medical press.

It may be helpful to know that in the USA, the FDA (Federal Drug Administration) classifies medicines in pregnancy in five groups:

A =	Studies show no risk, so harm to the unborn child appears only a remote possibility
B =	Animal and human studies indicate a lack of risk, but are not fully conclusive
C =	Animal studies indicate a risk, but there is no safety date in humans
D =	A definite risk exists, but the benefit may outweigh the risk in some people
X =	The risk outweighs any possible benefit

Zaleplon is classified as 'C' and zolpidem is 'B'. Zopiclone not classified as it is not available in the USA. There is no evidence of a teratogenic effect, and animal tests show a low risk of danger but you should still seek personal advice from your GP, who may then, if necessary, seek further specialist advice. Occasional use of a low dose would probably be of a low risk.

Chloral is classified as 'C'. There is no evidence of a teratogenic effect, but some problems have been reported and so you should seek personal advice from your GP, who may then, if necessary, seek further specialist advice. Clomethiazole is not classified, as it is not available in the USA. There is no evidence of a teratogenic effect, and animal tests show a low risk of danger, but some problems have been reported, so you should seek personal advice from your GP, who may then, if necessary, seek further specialist advice.

Will I need a blood test?

You will not need to have a blood test to check on your hypnotic.

Can I drive while I am taking them?

These hypnotics can reduce your ability to carry out skilled tasks, such as driving or operating machinery. You may also feel drowsy the day after you take them, especially if you then drink alcohol. Until these effects wear off or you know how your drug affects you, do not drive or operate machinery. You should take extra care, as they may affect your reaction times, even though you may feel well.

It is an offence to drive, to attempt to drive, or to be in charge of a vehicle when unfit through drugs. This would include sleeping tablets. It is advisable to let your insurance company know if you are taking these drugs. If you do not and you have an accident, it could affect your insurance cover.

If you are advised by your doctor not to drive, and continue to do so, the General Medical Council has advised doctors to inform the DVLA. The DVLA may then carry out an enquiry.

Treatments for psychosis and schizophrenia

Drugs known as antipsychotics or neuroleptics (often incorrectly known as the 'major tranquillisers')

Drug class: Phenothiazines, butyrophenones, thioxanthenes, and others

Drugs available	Brand name(s)	Forms available			
		Tablets	Capsules	Liquid	Injection
Phenothiazines					
Chlorpromazine [1]	Largactil®	✔		✔	✔
Fluphenazine	Moditen® Modecate®	✔			Depot
Methotrimeprazine or levomepromazine [3]	Nozinan®	✔			
Pericyazine	Neulactil®	✔		✔	
Perphenazine	Fentazin®	✔			
Pipothiazine	Piportil®				Depot
Promazine	Sparine®	✔		✔	
Thioridazine	Melleril®	✔		✔	
Trifluoperazine	Stelazine®	✔	✔	✔	✔
Thioxanthenes					
Flupentixol	Depixol®	✔			Depot
Zuclopenthixol	Clopixol®	✔			Depot
Butyrophenones					
Benperidol	Anquil®	✔			
Haloperidol	Haldol® Serenace® Haldol Decanoate®	✔	✔	✔	✔ and Depot
Others					
Fluspirilene	Redeptin®				Depot
Loxapine	Loxapac®		✔		
Pimozide	Orap®	✔			

1. Chlorpromazine is also available as suppositories.
2. Clozapine ('Clozaril®'), amisulpride, ('Solian®'), olanzapine ('Zyprexa®'), quetiapine ('Seroquel®'), risperidone ('Risperdal®'), sulpiride and zotepine ('Zoleptil®') have separate sections in this book.
3. Methotrimeprazine changed its name to levomepromazine as from 1998, although both are still in use.
4. Thioridazine is now restricted. Because of concerns about an effect on the heart called QTc prolongation, thioridazine is now only licensed for the treatment for schizophrenia in adults where another drug has failed. Treatment should be supervised by a consultant psychiatrist, there must be regular heart and blood monitoring, particular care in people with risk factors for heart disease and, if stopped, it is recommended that this be done slowly over one to two weeks.

For what are they used?

These drugs are generally used to help treat illnesses or conditions, such as psychosis, schizophrenia, and hypomania. They can also be used to help manage confusion, dementia, behaviour problems, and personality disorders. They are often known as 'neuroleptics', 'antipsychotic drugs', or, wrongly, as 'major tranquillisers'. They may also be used in smaller doses to help treat anxiety, tension, and agitation. Some of them are used to treat dizziness, nausea, and vomiting. Due to concerns about effects on the heart, thioridazine ('Melleril®') is now only available for the treatment of schizophrenia, along with specialist monitoring.

How do they work?

There is a naturally occurring chemical ('neurotransmitter') in the brain called dopamine. Dopamine is the chemical messenger mainly involved with thinking, emotions, behaviour, and perception. In some illnesses, dopamine may be overactive and upset the normal balance of chemicals in the brain. Excess dopamine helps to produce some of the symptoms of the illness. The main effect that these drugs have is to block some dopamine receptors, reducing the effect of having too much dopamine, and correcting the imbalance. This reduces the symptoms caused by having too high a level of dopamine in the brain.

How should I take them?

Tablets and capsules:

Tablets and capsules should be swallowed with at least half a glass of water while sitting or standing. This is to ensure that they reach the stomach and do not stick in the throat.

'Stelazine Spansules®' (trifluoperazine-modified release capsules) should be swallowed whole and not chewed. This is because the product is made to release the drug over a slightly longer period of time. This can help reduce the number of side-effects and allow your medicine to be taken fewer times a day. Crushing or chewing these capsules will cause the drug to be released too quickly.

Liquids:

Your pharmacist should give you a medicine spoon, dropper, or oral syringe. Use it carefully to measure the correct amount. Ask your pharmacist for a medicine spoon, if you do not have one.

Shake the bottle well before use, as the drug can settle to the bottom, and result in you receiving too low a dose at the start and too high a dose at the end of the bottle.

'Stelazine®' syrup (trifluoperazine) may be diluted in a drink of water or orange juice if necessary.

Suppositories:

Chlorpromazine ('Largactil®') is available as suppositories. Suppositories are specially shaped so that they can be inserted into the anus (the rectum or back passage). After removing a suppository from its wrapping, you should insert it as deeply as possible into your anus. You may find it easier to insert if you put one foot on a chair, or lie on your side with one leg drawn up as high as possible under the chin. Do not swallow them. If you have any problems using your suppositories ask your pharmacist or doctor for advice.

Injections:

It is sometimes necessary or helpful for these drugs to be given as 'depot' injections. A 'depot' injection is a long-acting injection, usually given into a buttock or sometimes the thigh. The injection releases the drug over several weeks, so you will not have to remember to take tablets at regular times each day. Depot injections are neither more nor less effective than tablets or capsules. If you are in hospital, a nurse will give the injection. Outside hospital, it may be given by a community psychiatric nurse, as a day patient, by your general practitioner, or the community nurse. You may need to have this injection every few weeks for some time. Initially, you will be given a 'test dose' to make sure the drug suits you. Then, if there are no problems, five to ten days later you will be given your first full dose injection, which will then be repeated every one to four weeks. These injections are usually given into the buttock, although some may be given into the thigh.

When should I take them?

Take your medication as directed on the medicine label. Try to take them at regular times each day. Taking them at mealtimes may make it easier for you to remember, as there is no problem about taking any of these drugs with or after food. If the instructions say to take them **once** a day, this is better at bedtime, as they may make you drowsy at first, but they are not sleeping tablets.

How long will they take to work?

Some of the effects of these drugs appear soon after taking them, for example, the drowsiness. The most important action, to help the symptoms of your illness, may take weeks or even months of regular medication to become fully effective. Equally, if your dose or treatment is changed, it may take a similarly long period before you notice the effects of such a change.

For how long will I need to keep taking them?

This should be discussed with your doctor, as people's responses are different. However, you will probably need to continue your treatment for a long time, possibly several years after your symptoms have disappeared, to make sure you are fully recovered from your illness. Long-term treatment should be reviewed at regular intervals, for example, every three to six months, or even sooner if there are problems.

Are they addictive?

These drugs are not really addictive. If you have taken them for a long time, you may experience some mild effects, such as nausea, restlessness, sweating, headache, or a runny nose, if you stop them suddenly. The main problems would be your symptoms returning.

Can I stop taking them suddenly?

It is unwise to stop taking them suddenly, even if you feel better. Your symptoms can return if treatment is stopped too early. This may occur some weeks, or even many months after the drug has been stopped and you may feel well before this happens. You could also experience mild withdrawal symptoms (as explained above). When the time comes, your doctor will usually withdraw the drug by a gradual reduction in the dose taken over a period of several weeks. You should discuss this fully with your doctor.

What sort of side-effects might occur?

Side-effect	What happens	What to do about it
Common		
Drowsiness	Feeling sleepy or sluggish. This can last for a few hours or longer after taking your dose	Do not drive or use machinery. Ask your doctor if you can take your antipsychotic at a different time of day. Your doctor may consider changing your dose or drug
Movement disorders (extrapyramidal or Parkinsonian side-effects)	Having shaky hands and feeling shaky. Your neck may twist back. Your eyes and tongue may move on their own. You may feel very restless	It is not usually dangerous and is a well known side-effect. If it is distressing or worries you, tell your doctor. He/she may be able to give you something for it, e.g. an anticholinergic drug, or perhaps try a different drug. Although it sometimes looks like Parkinson's disease, it is not the same thing
Constipation	Feeling 'blocked up' inside. You cannot pass a motion (stool)	This should wear off after a few weeks. Make sure you eat enough fibre, bran, or fruit, are drinking enough fluid, and that you keep active and take plenty of exercise, e.g. walking. If this does not help, ask your doctor or pharmacist for a mild laxative
Dry mouth	Not enough saliva or spit	Suck boiled sweets or wine gums (but be careful if you are putting on weight). This should wear off after a few weeks. If it is still troublesome, your doctor may be able to give you a mouth spray
Blurred vision	Things look fuzzy and you cannot focus properly	Do not drive with blurred vision. This should wear off after a few weeks. See your doctor about this if it does not wear off. He/she may be able to adjust your dose. You will not need glasses
Weight gain	Eating more and putting on weight	A diet high in vegetables and fibre may help prevent weight gain. See also a separate question in this section
Fairly common		
Raised prolactin (hyperprolactin-aemia)	In women, it can affect their breasts, which become bigger, and cause irregular periods, or cause impotence and chest changes in men and possibly even osteoporosis if taken over many years	It is not usually serious, but can be very distressing. Discuss with your doctor at your next appointment. He/she may want to adjust your drug or dose, as there may be long-term effects from raised prolactin
Restlessness or akathisia	Being on edge. You may perspire a lot or want to move around	Try and relax by taking deep breaths. Wear loose-fitting clothes. Discuss this with your doctor at your next appointment
Uncommon		
Hypotension	Low blood pressure. You may feel faint when you stand up	This may be more common with some drugs, e.g. the phenothiazines. Try not to stand up too quickly. If you feel dizzy, do not drive. Discuss with your doctor at your next appointment
Palpitations	A fast heart beat	It is not usually dangerous and can easily be treated if it lasts a long time
Sexual dysfunction	Difficulty in having an orgasm. No desire for sex	Discuss with your doctor. See also a separate question in this section

Side-effect	What happens	What to do about it
Rare		
QT or QTc prolongation	A slight change in the heart's electrical beat	You will not be aware of this, but you may need a heart test (ECG) at some time
Photosensitivity	Becoming blotchy in the sun	This can be common with chlorpromazine (see below). Avoid direct sunlight or sun lamps. Use a high factor sun block cream
Skin rashes	Blotches seen anywhere	Stop taking the drug and see your doctor now
Urinary retention	Not passing much urine	Contact your doctor now. This can be treated
Agranulocytosis	Low numbers of white cells in the blood. You may catch more infections	Tell your doctor if you have a sore throat, fever, or just feel ill. You may need a blood test

Table adapted from UK Psychiatric Pharmacy Group leaflets, with kind permission (www.ukppg.org.uk)

*If you are taking chlorpromazine ('Largactil®') you should avoid direct sunlight on your skin. This drug makes the skin extra-sensitive to sunlight and may cause it to redden and burn very easily. If you do go out in the sun, make sure you put on a high factor sunscreen first. Sun beds and sun lamps are also likely to cause a reaction and should be avoided.

Different drugs within these groups will have different degrees of side-effects.

Do not worry about this list of side-effects, as you may not experience any. There are other rare side-effects. If you develop any unusual symptoms, ask your doctor about these at your next appointment.

What should I do if I forget to take them?

Start again as soon as you remember unless it is nearly time for your next dose, then take the next dose as normal. Do not try to catch up by taking two or more doses at once, as you may experience more side-effects. You should tell your doctor about this at your next appointment. If you have problems remembering your doses (as many people do) ask your pharmacist, doctor, or nurse about this. There are special packs, boxes, and devices available that can be used to help you remember.

Will they make me drowsy?

These drugs may make you feel drowsy or sleepy. You should not drive (see below) or operate machinery until you know how they affect you. You should take extra care, as they may affect your reaction times or reflexes. They are not sleeping tablets, although if you take them at night they may help you to sleep.

Will they cause weight gain?

Weight gain with the phenothiazines is quite possible. Of the people who gain weight, most is gained during the first 6–12 months of treatment. It then tends to level out. It is thought that because these drugs cause increased appetite, you eat more and put on weight. It is not possible to say what the effect on your weight may be because each person is affected differently. All the phenothiazines seem to have similar effects, but these seem to be less with some of the other drugs. If you do start to put on weight, or have other problems with your weight, you should tell your doctor. He/she may be able to adjust your drug or the dose of your drug to reduce this effect. Your doctor can also arrange for you to see a dietician for advice. If you do gain weight, it is possible to lose it while you are still taking this medication, with expert advice about diet. In some people this can be a serious problem. If it causes you distress make sure your doctor knows about it. It is not thought that the other drugs cause major changes in weight, although a small weight change is possible.

Will it affect my sex life?

Drugs can affect desire (libido), arousal (erection), and orgasmic ability. Phenothiazines have been reported to have an adverse effect on all these three stages, partly through causing drowsiness and partly by other means. Thioridazine may be the worse drug for this. Generally, the other drugs in this section have lesser effects, e.g. the butyrophenones and thioxanthenes. If this happens, you should discuss it with your doctor, as a change in dose or drug may help to minimise the problem.

Can I drink alcohol while I am taking these drugs?

If you drink alcohol while taking these drugs, it may make you feel sleepier. This is particularly important if you need to drive or operate machinery, and you must seek advice on this.

Are there any foods or drinks that I should avoid?

You should have no problems with food or drinks other than alcohol (see above).

Will they affect my other medication?

Problems with other medications are uncommon, although a few have been recorded. The phenothiazines can interact with a few drugs, including some antidepressants and anticonvulsants, although your doctor should know about these. Other medicines, e.g. the painkiller co-proxamol, and some antihistamines can make you drowsy. When combined with your phenothiazine, this could make you even drowsier. This does not necessarily mean the drugs cannot be used together, just that you may need to follow your doctor's instructions very carefully. You should tell your doctor before starting or stopping these or any other drugs. Make sure your doctor knows about all the medicines you are taking.

If I am taking a contraceptive pill, will this be affected?

It is not thought that the contraceptive pill is affected by any of these drugs.

What if I want to start a family or discover I'm pregnant?

It is important to consider that there will be a risk to you and your child from taking a medicine during pregnancy, but also a possible risk from stopping the medicine, e.g. suffering a relapse. Unfortunately, no decision is risk-free. It will be for you to decide which is the least risk. All we can do here is to help you understand some of the issues, so you can make an informed decision. For your information, major malformations occur 'spontaneously' in about 2–4% of all pregnancies, even if no drugs are taken. The main problem with medicines is termed 'teratogenicity', i.e. a medicine causing a malformation in the unborn child. A medicine causing teratogenicity is called a 'teratogen'. Since a baby has completed its main development between days 17 and 60 of the pregnancy (the so-called 'first trimester'), these first 2–16 weeks are the main concern. After that, there may be other problems, e.g. some medicines may cause slower growth. The infant may also be affected after birth, e.g. withdrawal effects are possible with some drugs.

If possible, the best option is to plan in advance. If you think you could become pregnant, discuss this with your doctor and it may be possible to switch to medicines thought to carry least risk, and take other risk-reducing steps, e.g. adjusting doses, taking vitamin supplements, etc. If you have just discovered you are pregnant, don't panic, but, if possible, seek advice from your GP within the next few days. He or she may also want to refer you on to someone with more specialist knowledge of your medicine.

Very few medicines have been shown to be completely safe in pregnancy, so no manufacturer or advisor can ever say any medicine is safe. They will usually advise not to take a medicine during pregnancy, unless the benefit is much greater than the risk. In the UK, there is the NTIS (National Teratology Information Service) which offers individual risk assessments. However, its advice should always be used to help you and your doctor decide what is the risk to you and your baby. There is a risk from taking the medicine and a risk should you stop a medicine, e.g. you might become ill again and need to go back on the medication. The advice offered here is just that—**advice**, but may give you some idea about the possible risks and what (at the time of writing) is known through the medical press.

It may be helpful to know that in the USA, the FDA (Federal Drug Administration) classifies medicines in pregnancy in five groups:

A =	Studies show no risk, so harm to the unborn child appears only a remote possibility
B =	Animal and human studies indicate a lack of risk, but are not fully conclusive
C =	Animal studies indicate a risk, but there is no safety date in humans
D =	A definite risk exists, but the benefit may outweigh the risk in some people
X =	The risk outweighs any possible benefit

The phenothiazines available in the USA are all classified as 'C'. There has been some research on the use of phenothiazines in pregnancy, but mostly only with low doses. This research showed a risk of problems that was about twice that of women not taking such drugs (one in 30 with problems, one in 60 without). Occasional problems of sleepiness and drowsiness in the newborn have been reported. One piece of good news is that, in one study of women who took phenothiazines during pregnancy, the children's development was normal at 2 and 7 years old. You should, however, still seek personal advice from your GP, who may then, if necessary, seek further specialist advice.

Haloperidol is classified as 'C'. There is no proven evidence of a teratogenic effect, and animal tests show a low risk of danger. Some problems have, however, been reported and so you should seek personal advice from your GP, who may then, if necessary, seek further specialist advice.

Flupenthixol and zuclopenthixol are not classified, as they are not available in the USA. There is no evidence of a teratogenic effect, and animal tests show a low risk of danger. Some problems have, however, been reported and so you should seek personal advice from your GP, who may then, if necessary, seek further specialist advice.

Will I need a blood test?

Not usually. Some people who take higher doses occasionally need a blood test, e.g. to check on prolactin levels, or check your potassium levels if taking thioridazine.

Can I drive while I am taking them?

These drugs can affect your driving in two ways. Firstly, you may feel drowsy and/or suffer from blurred vision when starting to take any of these drugs. Secondly, the drugs can slow down your reactions or reflexes. This is especially true if you also have a dry mouth, blurred vision, or constipation (the so-called 'anticholinergic side-effects'). Until these wear off or you know how your drug affects you, do not drive or operate machinery. You should take extra care, as they may affect your reaction times or reflexes, even though you feel well.

It is an offence to drive, to attempt to drive, or to be in charge of a vehicle when unfit through drugs. It is advisable to let your insurance company know if you are taking these drugs. If you do not and you have an accident, it could affect your insurance cover.

If you are advised by your doctor not to drive, and continue to do so, the General Medical Council has advised doctors to inform the DVLA. The DVLA may then carry out an enquiry.

Drug: Risperidone

Drugs available	Brand name(s)	Forms available			
		Tablets	Capsules	Liquid	Injection
Risperidone	Risperdal® Risperdal Consta®	✔		✔	Long-acting injection

For what is risperidone used?

Risperidone is generally used to help treat illnesses or conditions, such as psychosis, schizophrenia, and hypomania. It can also be used to help confusion, dementia, behaviour problems, and personality disorders. It is often known as a 'neuroleptic', an 'antipsychotic', or, wrongly, as a 'major tranquilliser'. Smaller doses can be used to help treat anxiety, tension, and agitation, especially in older people.

Due to a slight increase in strokes, risperidone is no longer recommended for treating aggression and agitation in elderly people with demential. There is, however, no evidence of an increase in strokes in elderly people without dementia, nor in younger people.

How does risperidone work?

There is a naturally occurring chemical ('neurotransmitter') in the brain called dopamine. Dopamine is the chemical messenger mainly involved with thinking, emotions, behaviour, and perception. In some illnesses, dopamine may be overactive and upset the normal balance of chemicals. Excess dopamine helps to produce some of the symptoms of the illness. The main effect of risperidone is to block some dopamine receptors, reducing the effect of excess dopamine and correcting the imbalance. This reduces the symptoms caused by too much dopamine. Risperidone also has an effect on some serotonin (5-HT) receptors in the brain.

How should I take risperidone?

Tablets:

Tablets should be swallowed with at least half a glass of water while sitting or standing. This is to ensure that they reach the stomach and do not stick in the throat.

Syrup:

Your pharmacist should give you a medicine spoon, dropper, or oral syringe. Use it carefully to measure the correct amount. Ask your pharmacist for a medicine spoon if you do not have one. You may want to dilute the syrup with fruit juice if you do not like its taste.

Injections:

It is sometimes necessary or helpful for these drugs to be given as long-acting (sometimes called depot) injections. A long-acting injection is usually given into a buttock, or sometimes the thigh. Risperidone Consta® injection releases the medicine over several weeks, so you will not have to remember to take tablets at regular times each day. Injections like this are no more or less effective than the tablets. If you are in hospital, it will be given to you by a nurse. Outside hospital, it may be given to you by a community psychiatric nurse as a day patient, or by your GP or community nurse. You may need to have this injection every few weeks for some time. The risperidone injection releases only a little of the drug to start with then, about three weeks later, releases risperidone into your body over 2–4 weeks. Because of this delay, you may also need to take tablets for a few weeks after you start this injection, and the effects will last 6–7 weeks after your last injection.

When should I take risperidone?

Take your medication as directed on the medicine label. Try to take it at regular times each day. Taking it at mealtimes may make it easier for you to remember, as there is no problem about taking risperidone with or after food. If the instructions say to take it **once** a day, this is usually better at bedtime, as it may make you drowsy when you first start taking it, although it is not a sleeping tablet.

How long will risperidone take to work?

Some of the effects of risperidone appear soon after taking it, for example the drowsiness. The most important action, to help the symptoms of your illness, may take weeks, or even months of regular medication to become fully effective. Similarly, if your dose or treatment is changed, it may take an equally long period of time before you notice the effects of such a change.

For how long will I need to keep taking risperidone?

This should be discussed with your doctor as people's responses are different. However, you will probably need to continue your treatment for a long time, possibly several years after your symptoms have disappeared, to make sure you are fully over your illness. Long-term treatment should be reviewed at regular intervals, for example, every three to six months or even sooner if there are problems.

Is risperidone addictive?

Risperidone is not really addictive. If you have taken it for a long time you may experience mild effects if you stop taking it suddenly. The main problem would be your symptoms returning.

What sort of side-effects might occur?

Side-effect	What happens	What to do about it
Common		
Hypotension	A low blood pressure— this can make you feel dizzy	Try not to stand up too quickly. If you feel dizzy, do not drive. This dizziness is not dangerous
Headache	When your head is painful and pounding	You can take aspirin or paracetamol
Restlessness or akathisia	Being on edge. You may perspire a lot or want to move around	Try and relax by taking deep breaths. Wear loose-fitting clothes. Discuss this with your doctor at your next appointment
Uncommon		
Movement disorders (extra-pyramidal side-effects)	Having shaky hands and feeling shaky. Your neck may twist back, your eyes and tongue may move on their own, and you may feel very restless	It is not usually dangerous, but is a well known side-effect, particularly at higher doses, e.g. above 6mg a day of risperidone. If it is distressing or worries you, tell your doctor. He/she may be able to give you something for it, e.g. an anticholinergic drug or perhaps try a different drug. Although it sometimes looks like Parkinson's disease, it is not the same thing
Raised prolactin (hyperprolactin-aemia)	It can affect breasts and periods in women, or cause impotence and chest changes in men and possibly even osteoporosis if prolaction is raised for a long time	It is not usually serious, but can be very distressing. Discuss with your doctor at your next appointment. He/she may need to adjust your drug or reduce the dose
Drowsiness	Feeling sleepy or sluggish. It can last for a few hours after taking your dose	Do not drive or use machinery. Ask your doctor if you can take your risperidone at a different time
Weight gain	Eating more and putting on weight	A diet high in vegetables and fibre may help prevent weight gain. See also a separate question in this section
Constipation	Feeling blocked up inside. You cannot pass a motion	Make sure you include enough fibre, bran, and fruit in your diet and that you are drinking enough fluid. Keep active and take sufficient exercise, e.g. walking. If this does not help, ask your doctor or pharmacist for a mild laxative
Rare		
Blurred vision	Things look fuzzy and you cannot focus properly	Do not drive. See your doctor if you are worried. You will not need glasses
Sexual dysfunction	Finding it hard to have an orgasm. No desire for sex	Discuss with your doctor. See also a separate question in this section
Skin rashes	Blotches seen anywhere	**Stop taking the risperidone**—see your doctor now
Palpitations	A rapid heartbeat	It is not dangerous and can easily be treated if it lasts for a long time.

Table adapted from UK Psychiatric Pharmacy Group leaflets, with kind permission (www.ukppg.org.uk)

Do not worry about this list of side-effects, as you may not experience any. There are other rare side-effects. If you develop any unusual symptoms, ask your doctor about these at your next appointment.

Can I stop taking risperidone suddenly?

It is unwise to stop taking risperidone suddenly, even if you feel better. Your symptoms can return if treatment is stopped too early. This may occur some weeks, or even many months after the drug has been stopped. When the time comes, your doctor will usually withdraw the drug by a gradual reduction in the dose taken over a period of several weeks. You should discuss this fully with your doctor.

What should I do if I forget to take it?

Start again as soon as you remember unless it is nearly time for your next dose, and then take the next dose as normal. Do not try to catch up by taking two or more doses at once, as you may experience more side-effects. You should tell your doctor about this at your next appointment. If you have problems remembering your doses (as many people do) ask your pharmacist, doctor, or nurse about this. There are special packs, boxes, and devices available that can be used to help you remember.

Will risperidone make me drowsy?

Risperidone may make you feel drowsy or sleepy, although this is not common. You should not drive (see below) or operate machinery until you know how it affects you. You should take extra care, as it may affect your reaction times or reflexes.

Will risperidone cause weight gain?

Weight gain with risperidone is quite possible. Of the people who gain weight, most is gained during the first 6–12 months of treatment. It then tends to level out. It is not possible to say what the effect on your weight may be because each person will be affected differently. If you do start to put on weight, or have other problems with your weight, you should tell your doctor. He/she may be able to adjust your drug or the dose of your drug to reduce this effect. Your doctor can also arrange for you to see a dietician for advice. If you do gain weight it is possible to lose it while you are still taking this medication, with expert advice about diet. In some people this can be a serious problem. If it causes you distress make sure your doctor knows about it.

Will risperidone affect my sex life?

Drugs can affect desire (libido), arousal (erection), and orgasmic ability. Risperidone has been reported to have minor adverse effect on all three stages. If this happens, you should discuss it with your doctor, as a change in dose may help minimise the problem.

Can I drink alcohol while I am taking risperidone?

If you drink alcohol while taking risperidone, it may make you feel sleepier. This is particularly important if you need to drive or operate machinery, and you must seek advice on this.

Are there any foods or drinks that I should avoid?

You should have no problems with foods or drinks other than alcohol (see above).

Will risperidone affect my other medication?

You should have no problems if you take other medications.

If I am taking a contraceptive pill, will this be affected?

It is not thought that 'the pill' is affected by risperidone.

What if I want to start a family or discover I'm pregnant?

It is important to consider that there will be a risk to you and your child from taking a medicine during pregnancy, but also a possible risk from stopping the medicine, e.g. suffering a relapse. Unfortunately, no decision is risk-free. It will be for you to decide which is the least risk. All we can do here is to help you understand some of the issues, so you can make an informed decision. For your information, major malformations occur 'spontaneously' in about 2–4% of all pregnancies, even if no drugs are taken. The main problem with medicines is termed 'teratogenicity', i.e. a medicine causing a malformation in the unborn child. A medicine causing teratogenicity is called a 'teratogen'. Since a baby has completed its main development between days 17 and 60 of the pregnancy (the so-called 'first trimester'), these first 2–16 weeks are the main concern. After that, there may be other problems, e.g. some medicines may cause slower growth. The infant may also be affected after birth, e.g. withdrawal effects are possible with some drugs.

If possible, the best option is to plan in advance. If you think you could become pregnant, discuss this with your doctor and it may be possible to switch to medicines thought to carry least risk, and take other risk-reducing steps, e.g. adjusting doses, taking vitamin supplements, etc. If you have just discovered you are pregnant, don't panic, but, if possible, seek advice from your GP within the next few days. He or she may also want to refer you on to someone with more specialist knowledge of your medicine.

Very few medicines have been shown to be completely safe in pregnancy, so no manufacturer or advisor can ever say any medicine is safe. They will usually advise not to take a medicine during pregnancy, unless the benefit is much greater than the risk. In the UK, there is the NTIS (National Teratology Information Service) which offers individual risk assessments. However, its advice should always be used to help you and your doctor decide what is the risk to you and your baby. There is a risk from taking the medicine and a risk should you stop a medicine, e.g. you might become ill again and need to go back on the medication. The advice offered here is just that—**advice**, but may give you some idea about the possible risks and what (at the time of writing) is known through the medical press.

It may be helpful to know that in the USA, the FDA (Federal Drug Administration) classifies medicines in pregnancy in five groups:

A =	Studies show no risk, so harm to the unborn child appears only a remote possibility
B =	Animal and human studies indicate a lack of risk, but are not fully conclusive
C =	Animal studies indicate a risk, but there is no safety date in humans
D =	A definite risk exists, but the benefit may outweigh the risk in some people
X =	The risk outweighs any possible benefit

Risperidone is classified as 'C'. There are a few published reports of risperidone in pregnancy, and no problems were shown. You should, however, still seek personal advice from your GP, who may then, if necessary, seek further specialist advice.

Will I need a blood test?

Not usually. Some people who need to take higher doses occasionally need a blood test.

Can I drive while I am taking risperidone?

Risperidone may make you feel drowsy. Until this wears off or you know how your drug affects you, do not drive or operate machinery. You should take extra care, as it may affect your reaction times or reflexes, even if you feel well.

It is an offence to drive, to attempt to drive, or to be in charge of a vehicle when unfit through drugs. It is advisable to let your insurance company know if you are taking these drugs. If you do not, and you have an accident, it could affect your insurance cover.

If you are advised by your doctor not to drive, and continue to do so, the General Medical Council has advised doctors to inform the DVLA. The DVLA may then carry out an enquiry.

Drugs: Benzamides (or substituted benzamides)

Drugs available	Brand name(s)	Forms available			
		Tablets	Capsules	Liquid	Injection
Amisulpride	Solian®	✔		✔	
Sulpiride	Dolmatil® Sulpitil® Sulpor®	✔		✔	

For what are these drugs used?

These drugs are generally used to help treat illnesses or conditions, such as psychosis, schizophrenia, and hypomania. They can also be used to help confusion, dementia, behaviour problems, and personality disorders. They are often known as 'neuroleptics', 'antipsychotic drugs', or, wrongly, as 'major tranquillisers'.

How do they work?

There is a naturally occurring chemical ('neurotransmitter') in the brain called dopamine. Dopamine is the chemical messenger mainly involved with thinking, emotions, behaviour, and perception. In some illnesses, dopamine may be overactive and upsets the normal balance of chemicals. This excess dopamine helps to produce some of the symptoms of the illness. The main effect that these drugs have is to block dopamine receptors in the brain, reducing the effect of having too much dopamine, and correcting the imbalance. This reduces the symptoms caused by having too much dopamine.

How should I take them?

Tablets:

Tablets should be swallowed with at least half a glass of water while sitting or standing. This is to make sure that they reach the stomach and do not stick in the throat.

Liquid:

Your pharmacist should give you a medicine spoon, dropper, or oral syringe. Use it carefully to measure the correct amount. Ask your pharmacist for a medicine spoon if you do not have one. Shake the bottle well before use.

When should I take them?

Take your medication as directed on the medicine label. Try to take them at regular times each day. Taking them at mealtimes may make it easier for you to remember, as there is no problem about taking any of these drugs with or after food. If the instructions say to take them **once** a day, this is usually better at bedtime, as they may make you drowsy at first, although they are not sleeping tablets.

How long will they take to work?

Some of the effects of these drugs appear soon after taking them, for example, drowsiness. However, the most important action, to help the symptoms of your illness, may take weeks or even months of regular medication to become fully effective. Similarly, if your dose or treatment is changed, it may take an equally long period of time before you notice the effects of such a change.

For how long will I need to keep taking them?

This should be discussed with your doctor as people's responses are different. You will probably need to continue your treatment for a long time, possibly several years after your symptoms have disappeared, to make sure you are fully over your illness. Long-term treatment should be reviewed at regular intervals, for example, every three to six months or even sooner if there are problems.

Are they addictive?

These drugs are not really addictive. If you have taken them for a long time you may experience some mild effects if you stop them suddenly. The main problem would be your symptoms returning.

Can I stop taking them suddenly?

It is unwise to stop taking them suddenly, even if you feel better. Your symptoms can return if treatment is stopped too early. This may occur some weeks or even many months after the drug has been stopped. You could also experience mild withdrawal symptoms (as explained above). When the time comes, your doctor will usually withdraw the drug by a gradual reduction in the dose taken over a period of several weeks. You should discuss this fully with your doctor.

What should I do if I forget to take them?

Start again as soon as you remember unless it is nearly time for your next dose, then take the next dose as normal. Do not try to catch up by taking two or more doses at once, as you may experience more side-effects. You should tell your doctor about this at your next appointment. If you have problems remembering your doses (as many people do) ask your pharmacist, doctor, or nurse about this. There are special packs, boxes, and devices available that can be used to help you to remember.

What sort of side-effects might occur?

Side-effect	What happens	What to do about it
Common		
Drowsiness	Feeling sleepy or sluggish. It can last for a few hours after taking your dose	Do not drive or use machinery. Ask your doctor if you can take your drug at a different time
Movement disorders (extra-pyramidal side-effects)	Having shaky hands and feeling shaky. Your neck may twist back. Your eyes and tongue may move on their own. You may feel very restless	It is not usually dangerous, but is a well known side-effect. If it is distressing or worries you, tell your doctor. He/she may be able to give you something for it, e.g. an anticholinergic drug or perhaps try a different drug. Although it sometimes looks like Parkinson's disease, it is not the same thing
Less common		
Hypotension	A low blood pressure—this can make you feel dizzy	Try not to stand up too quickly. If you feel dizzy, do not drive. This dizziness is not dangerous
Headache	When your head is painful and pounding	Take aspirin or paracetamol
Restlessness or akathisia	Being on edge. You may perspire more or want to move around	Try and relax by taking deep breaths. Wear loose-fitting clothes. Discuss this with your doctor at your next appointment
Raised prolactin (hyperprolactin-aemia)	It can affect breasts and periods in women, or cause impotence and chest changes in men or even osteoporosis if prolactin is raised for a long time	It is not usually serious, but can be very distressing. Discuss with your doctor at your next appointment; he or she may need to change your drug or reduce the dose
Constipation	Feeling 'blocked up' inside. You cannot pass a motion	Make sure you eat enough fibre, bran, or fruit and that you are drinking plenty of fluid. Keep active and take plenty of exercise, e.g. walking. If this does not help, ask your doctor or pharmacist for a mild laxative
Rare		
Blurred vision	Things look fuzzy and you cannot focus properly	Do not drive. See your doctor if you are worried. You will not need glasses
Weight gain	Eating more and putting on weight	A diet high in vegetables and fibre may help prevent weight gain. See also a separate question in this section
Sexual dysfunction	Finding it hard to have an orgasm. No desire for sex	Discuss with your doctor. See also a separate question in this section
Skin rashes	Blotches seen anywhere	**Stop taking** the tablets and see your doctor now

Table adapted from UK Psychiatric Pharmacy Group leaflets, with kind permission (www.ukppg.org.uk)

Do not worry about this list of side-effects, as you may not experience any. There are other rare side-effects. If you develop any unusual symptoms, ask your doctor about these at your next appointment.

Will they make me drowsy?

These drugs may make you feel drowsy or sleepy, although this is much less common than with many other similar drugs. You should not drive or operate machinery until you know how they affect you. You should take extra care, as they may affect your reaction times or reflexes. They are not sleeping tablets, although if you take them at night they may help you to sleep.

Will they cause weight gain?

Weight gain is uncommon with these drugs. It is, however, not possible to say what the effect on your own weight may be because each person will be affected differently. If you do start to put on weight or have other problems, you should tell your doctor. He/she may be able to adjust your drug or the dose of your drug, to reduce this effect. Your doctor can also arrange for you to see a dietician for advice. If you do gain weight, it is possible to lose it while you are still taking this medication, with expert advice about diet.

Will it affect my sex life?

Drugs can affect desire (libido), arousal (erection), and orgasmic ability. Sulpiride and amisulpride have not been reported to have a significant effect on these. If this happens, however, you should discuss it with your doctor, as a change in dose or drug may help to minimise the problem.

Can I drink alcohol while I am taking these drugs?

If you drink alcohol while taking these drugs, it may make you feel sleepier. This is particularly important if you need to drive or operate machinery, and you must seek advice on this.

Are there any foods, or drinks that I should avoid?

You should have no problems with any food or drink other than alcohol (see above).

Will they affect my other medication?

You should have no problems if you take other medications. You should always tell your doctor before starting or stopping this or any other drugs. Make sure your doctor knows about all the medicines you are taking.

If I am taking a contraceptive pill, will this be affected?

It is not thought that 'the pill' is affected by either of these drugs.

What if I want to start a family or discover I'm pregnant?

It is important to consider that there will be a risk to you and your child from taking a medicine during pregnancy, but also a possible risk from stopping the medicine, e.g. suffering a relapse. Unfortunately, no decision is risk-free. It will be for you to decide which is the least risk. All we can do here is to help you understand some of the issues, so you can make an informed decision. For your information, major malformations occur 'spontaneously' in about 2–4% of all pregnancies, even if no drugs are taken. The main problem with medicines is termed 'teratogenicity', i.e. a medicine causing a malformation in the unborn child. A medicine causing teratogenicity is called a 'teratogen'. Since a baby has completed its main development between days 17 and 60 of the pregnancy (the so-called 'first trimester'), these first 2–16 weeks are the main concern. After that, there may be other problems, e.g. some medicines may cause slower growth. The infant may also be affected after birth, e.g. withdrawal effects are possible with some drugs.

If possible, the best option is to plan in advance. If you think you could become pregnant, discuss this with your doctor and it may be possible to switch to medicines thought to carry least risk, and take other risk-reducing steps, e.g. adjusting doses, taking vitamin supplements, etc. If you have just discovered you are pregnant, don't panic, but, if possible, seek advice from your GP within the next few days. He or she may also want to refer you on to someone with more specialist knowledge of your medicine.

Very few medicines have been shown to be completely safe in pregnancy, so no manufacturer or advisor can ever say any medicine is safe. They will usually advise not to take a medicine during pregnancy, unless the benefit is much greater than the risk. In the UK, there is the NTIS (National Teratology Information Service) which offers individual risk assessments. However, its advice should always be used to help you and your doctor decide what is the risk to you and your baby. There is a risk from taking the medicine and a risk should you stop a medicine, e.g. you might become ill again and need to go back on the medication. The advice offered here is just that—**advice**, but may give you some idea about the possible risks and what (at the time of writing) is known through the medical press.

It may be helpful to know that in the USA, the FDA (Federal Drug Administration) classifies medicines in pregnancy in five groups:

A =	Studies show no risk, so harm to the unborn child appears only a remote possibility
B =	Animal and human studies indicate a lack of risk, but are not fully conclusive
C =	Animal studies indicate a risk, but there is no safety date in humans
D =	A definite risk exists, but the benefit may outweigh the risk in some people
X =	The risk outweighs any possible benefit

Sulpiride and amisulpride are not classified, as they are not available in the USA. There is no evidence of a teratogenic effect and animal tests show a low risk of danger. Some problems have, however, been reported and so you should seek personal advice from your GP, who may then, if necessary, seek further specialist advice.

Will I need a blood test?

Not usually.

Can I drive while I am taking them?

These drugs can affect your driving, e.g. you may feel drowsy. Until this wears off or you know how your drug affects you, do not drive or operate machinery. You should take extra care, as they may affect your reaction times or reflexes even if you feel well.

It is an offence to drive, to attempt to drive, or to be in charge of a vehicle when unfit through drugs. It is advisable to let your insurance company know if you are taking these drugs. If you do not and you have an accident, it could affect your insurance cover.

If you are advised by your doctor not to drive, and continue to do so, the General Medical Council has advised doctors to inform the DVLA. The DVLA may then carry out an enquiry.

Drugs: Olanzapine, quetiapine and zotepine

Drugs available	Brand name(s)	Forms available			
		Tablets	Capsules	Liquid	Injection
Olanzapine	Zyprexa®	✔		✔ (Dispersible tablets)	✔
Quetiapine	Seroquel®	✔			
Zotepine	Zoleptil®	✔			

For what are they used?

These drugs are generally used to help treat illnesses or conditions, such as psychosis and schizophrenia. Olanzapine and quetiapine can also be used to help treat mood disorders, such as hypomania.

How do they work?

There is a naturally occurring chemical ('neurotransmitter') in the brain called dopamine. Dopamine is the chemical messenger mainly involved with thinking, emotions, behaviour, and perception. In some illnesses, dopamine may be overactive and upset the normal balance of chemicals. Excess dopamine helps to produce some of the symptoms of the illness. The main effect of these drugs is to block some dopamine receptors in the brain, reducing the effect of having too much dopamine, and correcting the imbalance. This reduces the symptoms caused by having too much dopamine. These three drugs also have effects on other neurotransmitters, e.g. serotonin (5-HT), and their beneficial effects may be related to these.

How should I take them?

The tablets should be swallowed with at least half a glass of water while sitting or standing. This is to make sure that they reach the stomach and do not stick in the throat.

When should I take them?

Take your medication as directed on the medicine label. Try to take them at regular times each day. Taking them at mealtimes may make it easier for you to remember, as there is no problem about taking any of these drugs with or after food. If the instructions say to take them **once** a day, this is usually better at bedtime, as they may make you drowsy at first, but they are not sleeping tablets.

How long will they take to work?

Some of the effects of these drugs appear soon after taking them, for example, the drowsiness. The most important action, to help the symptoms of your illness, may take weeks, or even months of regular medication to become fully effective. Similarly, if your dose or treatment is changed, it may take an equally long period of time before you notice the effects of such a change.

For how long will I need to keep taking them?

This should be discussed with your doctor as people's responses are different. You will probably need to continue your treatment for a long time, possibly several years after your symptoms have disappeared, to make sure you have fully recovered from your illness. Long-term treatment should be reviewed at regular intervals, for example, every three to six months or even sooner if there are problems.

Are they addictive?

These drugs are not really addictive. If you have taken them for a long time, you may experience some mild effects if you stop taking them suddenly. The main problem would be your symptoms returning.

Can I stop taking them suddenly?

It is unwise to stop taking them suddenly, even if you feel better. Your symptoms can return if treatment is stopped too early. This may occur some weeks or even many months after the drug has been stopped. You could also experience mild withdrawal symptoms (as explained above). When the time comes, your doctor will usually withdraw the drug by a gradual reduction in the dose taken over a period of several weeks. You should discuss this fully with your doctor.

What should I do if I forget to take them?

Start again as soon as you remember unless it is nearly time for your next dose, then take the next dose as normal. Do not try to catch up by taking two or more doses at once, as you may experience more side-effects. You should tell your doctor about this at your next appointment. If you have problems remembering your doses (as many people do) ask your pharmacist, doctor, or nurse about this. There are some special packs, boxes, and devices available that can be used to help you remember.

Will they make me drowsy?

These drugs may make you feel drowsy or sleepy. You should not drive (see below) or operate machinery until you know how they affect you. You should take extra care, as they may affect your reaction times or reflexes. However, they are not sleeping tablets, although if you take them at night they may help you to sleep.

Will they cause weight gain?

Weight gain with these drugs is quite possible and more likely with olanzapine and zotepine. In the people who gain weight, most is gained during the first 6–12 months of treatment. It then tends to level out. It is not possible to say what the effect on your own weight may be because each person will be affected differently. If you do start to put on weight or have other problems, you should tell your doctor. He/she may be able to adjust your drug or the dose of your drug to reduce this effect. Your doctor can also arrange for you to see a dietician for advice. If you do gain weight, it is possible to lose it while you are still taking this medication, with expert advice about diet, but the sooner you seek help the better. In some people this can be a serious problem. If it causes you distress make sure your doctor knows about it.

Will it affect my sex life?

Drugs can affect desire (libido), arousal (erection), and orgasmic ability. Olanzapine and quetiapine are not thought to have a significant effect on any of these stages, but problems have been reported occasionally with zotepine. If this happens, however, you should discuss it with your doctor, as a change in dose or drug may help to minimise the problem.

Can I drink alcohol while I am taking these drugs?

If you drink alcohol while taking these drugs it may make you feel sleepier. This is particularly important if you need to drive or operate machinery, and you must seek advice on this.

Are there any foods or drinks that I should avoid?

You should have no problems with any food or drink other than alcohol (see above).

What sort of side-effects might occur?

Olanzapine:

Side-effect	What happens	What to do about it
Common		
Drowsiness	Feeling sleepy or sluggish. It can last for a few hours after taking your dose	Do not drive or use machinery. Ask your doctor if you can take your olanzapine at a different time
Weight gain	Eating more and putting on weight, especially just after you start the drug	A diet high in vegetables and fibre may help prevent weight gain. See also a separate question in this section
Uncommon		
Hypotension	A low blood pressure— this can make you feel dizzy, especially when you stand up	Try not to stand up too quickly. If you feel dizzy, do not drive. This dizziness is not dangerous
Dry mouth	Not much saliva or spit	Suck sugar-free boiled sweets. If it is severe, your doctor can give you a mouth spray
Constipation	Feeling 'blocked up' inside. You cannot pass a motion	Make sure you eat sufficient fibre, bran, or fruit and are drinking enough fluid. Keep active and take plenty of exercise, e.g. walking. If this does not help, ask your doctor or pharmacist for a mild laxative
Peripheral oedema	When your ankles swell up	Discuss with your doctor
Rare		
Diabetes	Feeling thirsty, drinking more, going to the toilet more	Olanzapine can effect blood sugar levels. If you suffer any of these symptoms, see your doctor within the next week or so
Altered liver function	Your liver is not working as normal. You should not feel any symptoms. This is only discovered if your doctor does a blood test	Continue to take your olanzapine. Your liver should return to normal eventually. Your doctor will probably want regular blood tests to make sure your liver is working properly. Serious liver problems do not occur with olanzapine, so do not worry too much
Photosensitivity	Skin goes blotchy in the sun	Avoid direct sunlight or sun-lamps. Use a high factor sun block cream

Table adapted from UK Psychiatric Pharmacy Group leaflets, with kind permission (www.ukppg.org.uk)

Quetiapine:

Side-effect	What happens	What to do about it
Common		
Hypotension	A low blood pressure— this can make you feel dizzy, especially when you stand up	Try not to stand up too quickly. If you feel dizzy, do not drive. This dizziness is not dangerous
Drowsiness	Feeling sleepy or sluggish. This can last for a few hours, or longer after taking your dose	Do not drive or use machinery. Ask your doctor if you can take your drug at a different time of day. Your doctor may be able to change your dose
Agitation	Feeling restless or on edge	Try and relax by taking deep breaths. Contact your doctor if it worries you
Stomach upset	This includes feeling and being sick, and diarrhoea	If it is mild, see your pharmacist. If it lasts for more than a day, see your doctor
Uncommon		
Weight gain	Eating more and putting on weight, especially just after you start the drug	A diet high in vegetables and fibre may help prevent weight gain. See also a separate question in this section
Anticholinergic side-effects	Dry mouth, blurred vision, difficulty in passing urine, constipation	These are usually mild and should wear off after a few weeks. If not, contact your doctor or pharmacist
Rare		
Headache	When your head is painful and pounding	Ask your pharmacist if it is safe to take aspirin or paracetamol with any other medicines you may be taking
Insomnia	Not being able to sleep at night	Discuss with your doctor. He/she may change the time of your dose

Table adapted from UK Psychiatric Pharmacy Group leaflets, with kind permission (www.ukppg.org.uk)

Zotepine:

Side-effect	What happens	What to do about it
Common		
Weight gain	Eating more and putting on weight	A diet high in vegetables and fibre may help prevent weight gain. See also a separate question in this section
Raised prolactin (hyperprolactin-aemia)	In women this can affect their breasts, which become bigger and cause irregular periods, or cause impotence and chest changes in men	Usually, it is not serious, but can be very distressing. Discuss with your doctor at your next appointment. He or she may need to reduce your dose or change to another drug
Movement disorders (extrapyramidal or Parkinsonian side-effects	Having shaky hands and feeling shaky. Your neck may twist back, your eyes and tongue may move on their own and you may feel very restless	It is not usually dangerous and is a well known side-effect. If it is distressing or worries you, tell your doctor. He/she may be able to give you something for it, e.g. an anticholinergic drug or perhaps try a different drug. Although it sometimes looks like Parkinson's disease, it is not the same thing
Drowsiness	Feeling sleepy or sluggish. This can last for a few hours or longer after taking your dose	Do not drive or use machinery. Ask your doctor if you can take your antipsychotic at a different time of day. Your doctor may change your dose or drug.
Dry mouth	Not enough saliva or spit	Suck boiled sweets or wine gums (but be careful if you are putting on weight). This should wear off after a few weeks. If it is still troublesome, your doctor may be able to give you a mouth spray
Constipation	Feeling 'blocked up inside'. You cannot pass a motion (stool)	This should wear off after a few weeks. Make sure you eat enough fibre, bran, or fruit, are drinking enough fluid, and that you keep active and take plenty of exercise, e.g. walking. If this does not help, ask your doctor or pharmacist for a mild laxative
Blurred vision	Things look fuzzy and you cannot focus properly	Do not drive with blurred vision. This should wear off after a few weeks. See your doctor about this if it does not wear off. He/she may be able to adjust your dose. You will not need glasses
Uncommon		
Hypotension	Low blood pressure. You may feel faint when you stand up	Try not to stand up too quickly. If you feel dizzy, do not drive. Discuss with your doctor at your next appointment
Palpitations	A fast heart beat	This is not usually dangerous and can easily be treated if it lasts a long time
Rare		
Seizures	Having a fit or convulsion	Stop taking zotepine and contact your doctor immediately

Table adapted from UK Psychiatric Pharmacy Group leaflets, with kind permission (www.ukppg.org.uk)

Do not worry about this list of side-effects, as you may not experience any. There are other rare side-effects. If you develop any unusual symptoms, ask your doctor about these at your next appointment.

Will they affect my other medication?

You should have no problems if you take other medications, although a few problems can occur. Sedative drugs might make you feel sleepier. This does not necessarily mean the drugs cannot be used together, just that you may need to follow your doctor's instructions very carefully. You should tell your doctor before starting or stopping these, or any other drugs. Make sure your doctor knows about all the medicines you are taking.

Will I need a blood test?

Not usually. It may be necessary to test for blood sugar or prolactin levels occasionally.

Can I drive while I am taking them?

These drugs can affect your driving, e.g. you may feel drowsy. Until this wears off or you know how your drug affects you, do not drive or operate machinery. You should take extra care, as they may affect your reaction times or reflexes, even though you feel well.

It is an offence to drive, to attempt to drive, or to be in charge of a vehicle when unfit through drugs. It is advisable to let your insurance company know if you are taking these drugs. If you do not and you have an accident, it could affect your insurance cover.

If you are advised by your doctor not to drive, and continue to do so, the General Medical Council has advised doctors to inform the DVLA. The DVLA may then carry out an enquiry.

If I am taking a contraceptive pill, will this be affected?

It is not thought that 'the pill' is affected by any of these drugs.

What if I want to start a family or discover I'm pregnant?

It is important to consider that there will be a risk to you and your child from taking a medicine during pregnancy, but also a possible risk from stopping the medicine, e.g. suffering a relapse. Unfortunately, no decision is risk-free. It will be for you to decide which is the least risk. All we can do here is to help you understand some of the issues, so you can make an informed decision. For your information, major malformations occur 'spontaneously' in about 2–4% of all pregnancies, even if no drugs are taken. The main problem with medicines is termed 'teratogenicity', i.e. a medicine causing a malformation in the unborn child. A medicine causing teratogenicity is called a 'teratogen'. Since a baby has completed its main development between days 17 and 60 of the pregnancy (the so-called 'first trimester'), these first 2–16 weeks are the main concern. After that, there may be other problems, e.g. some medicines may cause slower growth. The infant may also be affected after birth, e.g. withdrawal effects are possible with some drugs.

If possible, the best option is to plan in advance. If you think you could become pregnant, discuss this with your doctor and it may be possible to switch to medicines thought to carry least risk, and take other risk-reducing steps, e.g. adjusting doses, taking vitamin supplements, etc. If you have just discovered you are pregnant, don't panic, but, if possible, seek advice from your GP within the next few days. He or she may also want to refer you on to someone with more specialist knowledge of your medicine.

Very few medicines have been shown to be completely safe in pregnancy, so no manufacturer or advisor can ever say any medicine is safe. They will usually advise not to take a medicine during pregnancy, unless the benefit is much greater than the risk. In the UK, there is the NTIS (National Teratology Information Service) which offers individual risk assessments. However, its advice should always be used to help you and your doctor decide what is the risk to you and your baby. There is a risk from taking the medicine and a risk should you stop a medicine, e.g. you might become ill again and need to go back on the medication. The advice offered here is just that—**advice**, but may give you some idea about the possible risks and what (at the time of writing) is known through the medical press.

It may be helpful to know that in the USA, the FDA (Federal Drug Administration) classifies medicines in pregnancy in five groups:

A =	Studies show no risk, so harm to the unborn child appears only a remote possibility
B =	Animal and human studies indicate a lack of risk, but are not fully conclusive
C =	Animal studies indicate a risk, but there is no safety date in humans
D =	A definite risk exists, but the benefit may outweigh the risk in some people
X =	The risk outweighs any possible benefit

Olanzapine and quetiapine are both classified as 'C'. There is little human information available, but so far no problems have been published. Zotepine is not classified and the risk is unknown. You should, however, seek personal advice from your GP, who may then if necessary seek further specialist advice.

Drug: Clozapine

Drugs available	Brand name(s)	Forms available			
		Tablets	**Capsules**	**Liquid**	**Injection**
Clozapine	Clozaril® Denzapine® Zaponex®	✔			

For what is clozapine used?

Clozapine is an 'antipsychotic' or 'neuroleptic' drug used to treat the symptoms of schizophrenia in people who have not done well on at least two other similar drugs, e.g. who have not responded or who have had unpleasant side-effects.

How does clozapine work?

There are many naturally occurring chemical messengers ('neurotransmitters') in the brain. Two of these are called dopamine and serotonin. Dopamine is the chemical messenger mainly involved with thinking, emotions, and behaviour. In schizophrenia, it may be overactive and helps to produce some of the symptoms of the illness. The main effect that clozapine has is to block some of the dopamine and serotonin receptors in the brain, reducing the effect of having high levels, and reducing the symptoms caused by too much dopamine. The action of clozapine may also be related to several other neurotransmitters in the brain.

How should I take clozapine?

Clozapine tablets should be swallowed whole, with at least half a glass of water while sitting or standing. This is to ensure that they reach the stomach and do not stick in the throat.

When should I take clozapine?

Take your clozapine as directed on the medicine label. Try to take it at regular times each day. Taking it at mealtimes may make it easier to remember, as there is no problem in taking clozapine with or after food. If the instructions say to take it **once** a day, this should usually be at bedtime, as it may make you feel drowsy when first taking it, although clozapine is not a sleeping tablet.

How long will clozapine take to work?

Some effects of clozapine appear soon after taking it, for example the drowsiness. The most important action, helping to control the symptoms of your illness, may take several months or even up to a year of regular medication to become fully effective. In the same way, if your dose or treatment is changed, it may take an equally long time before you notice the effects of such a change.

For how long will I need to keep taking it?

This should be discussed with your doctor, as people's responses are different. However, you will probably need to continue your treatment for several years. Long-term treatment should be reviewed every three to six months, or sooner if there are problems. It is likely that you will benefit from clozapine by taking it for many years.

Is clozapine addictive?

Clozapine is not addictive.

Can I stop taking clozapine suddenly?

It is unwise to stop taking clozapine suddenly, even if you feel better. Your symptoms can return if treatment is stopped too early. This may occur some weeks or even many months after the drug has been stopped. If the clozapine has had an effect on your blood, it might be important to stop the tablets suddenly. Your doctor will discuss this with you.

What should I do if I forget to take it?

Start again as soon as you remember unless it is almost time for your next dose, then go on as before. Do not try to catch up by taking two or more doses at once, as you may experience more side-effects. You should tell your doctor about this at your next appointment. If you have problems remembering your doses (as many people do) ask your pharmacist, doctor, or nurse about this. There are special packs, boxes, and devices available that can be used to help you remember.

Will clozapine make me drowsy?

Clozapine may make you feel drowsy or sleepy. You should not drive (see *Page 149*) or operate machinery until you know how it affects you. You should take extra care, as it may affect your reaction times or reflexes. Clozapine is not, however, a sleeping tablet, although if you take it at night it may help you to sleep. If this drowsiness does not wear off, discuss it with your doctor. It may be possible to change your doses round.

Will clozapine cause weight gain?

When you start taking clozapine, you may experience weight gain. This tends to stop after a time, but can be a problem with clozapine. It is thought that the drug causes an increase in appetite, which then makes you eat more and put on weight. It is not possible to know what the effect on your own weight may be because each person will be affected differently. Unfortunately, many of the other drugs used for treating this illness seem to have this effect too, but some appear better than others. If you do start to put on weight, or have problems with your weight, you should tell your doctor. He/she may be able to change your clozapine dose to reduce this effect. Your doctor can also arrange for you to see a dietician for advice. If you do gain weight, it is possible to lose it while you are still taking this medication, with expert advice about diet, but the sooner you seek help the better. Make sure your doctor knows about this if it causes you distress.

If you do gain weight, it is possible to lose it while you are still taking this medication, with expert advice about diet, but the sooner you seek help the better.

Will clozapine affect my sex life?

Drugs can affect desire (libido), arousal (erection), and orgasmic ability. Unlike many other antipsychotic drugs, clozapine has not been reported as having a major adverse effect on the three stages, except by causing drowsiness. However, if this happens, you should discuss it with your doctor, who may recommend a change in dose to help minimise the problem.

Can I drink alcohol while I am taking clozapine?

You should avoid alcohol while taking clozapine, as it may make you feel sleepier. This is particularly important if you need to drive or operate machinery. You must seek advice on this.

Are there any foods or drinks that I should avoid?

You should have no problems with any food or drink other than alcohol (see above).

Will they affect my other medication?

You should have few problems if you take other medications, although some have been recorded. Clozapine should not be taken with some antibiotics, e.g. erythromycin, co-trimoxazole and chloramphenicol. It can also interact with a few other drugs, including some drugs for depression and some anticonvulsants, e.g. carbamazepine (Tegretol®), although your doctor should know about these. This does not necessarily mean the drugs cannot be used together, just that you may need to follow your doctor's instructions very carefully. Make sure your doctor knows about all the medicines you are taking. Some other medicines, e.g. the painkiller co-proxamol ('Distalgesic®') and some antihistamines (e.g. for hay fever) can make you drowsy. When combined with clozapine, this could make you even drowsier. Ask your pharmacist before buying any medicines over the counter, e.g. cimetidine. You should tell your doctor before starting or stopping these or any other drugs.

If I am taking a contraceptive pill, will this be affected?

It is not thought that the contraceptive pill is affected by clozapine. With many drugs of this type, a woman's periods may be irregular or even disappear. This is less likely with clozapine and so they may reappear or become more regular if changing to clozapine.

What sort of side-effects might occur?

Side-effect	What happens	What to do about it
Common		
Drowsiness	Feeling sleepy or sluggish. It can last for a few hours after taking your dose	Do not drive or use machinery. Ask your doctor if you can take your clozapine at a different time
Constipation	Feeling 'blocked up' inside. You cannot pass a motion	Make sure you eat enough fibre, bran, or fruit, and that you are drinking enough fluid, keep active and take sufficient exercise, e.g. walking. If this does not help, ask your doctor or pharmacist for a mild laxative
Hypersalivation	Your mouth is full of saliva or spit. You may drool; your pillow may be wet in the morning	This is not dangerous, but can be annoying or distressing. Your doctor may be able to give you a tablet (e.g. hyoscine) to help this. Some people find propping their head up on pillows at night also helps
Hypotension	Low blood pressure— this can make you feel dizzy	Try not to stand up too quickly. If you feel dizzy, do not drive. This dizziness is not dangerous
Weight gain	Eating more and putting on weight	A diet high in vegetables and fibre may help to prevent weight gain. See also a separate question in this section
Rare		
Movement disorders (extrapyramidal or Parkinsonian side-effects)	Having shaky hands and feeling shaky. Your neck may twist back. Your eyes and tongue may move on their own. You may feel very restless	It is not usually dangerous and is a well known, but rare side-effect. If it is distressing or worries you, tell your doctor. He/she may be able to give you something for it, e.g. an anticholinergic drug. Although it sometimes looks like Parkinson's disease, it is not the same thing
Fever or flu-like symptoms	A high temperature	Check with your doctor to make sure you do not have a blood problem. If you do not, try aspirin or paracetamol. Your pharmacist will be able to advise if these are safe to take with other drugs you may be taking. Always tell your doctor or carer if you suffer an unexpected fever, sore throat, or illness
Agranulocytosis or neutropenia	Low numbers of white cells in the blood. You may catch more infections	This will be picked up from your blood tests (see separate question in this section). It happens in about 2 or 3 in 100 people. Always tell your doctor or carer if you experience an unexpected fever, sore throat, or illness
Seizures	Having a fit or convulsion	Stop taking clozapine and contact your doctor immediately
Palpitations	A rapid heart beat	It is not dangerous and can easily be treated if it lasts for a long time

Table adapted from UK Psychiatric Pharmacy Group leaflets, with kind permission (www.ukppg.org.uk)

Do not worry about this list of side-effects, as you may not experience any. There are other rare side-effects. If you develop any unusual symptoms, ask your doctor about these at your next appointment.

What if I want to start a family or discover I'm pregnant?

It is important to consider that there will be a risk to you and your child from taking a medicine during pregnancy, but also a possible risk from stopping the medicine, e.g. suffering a relapse. Unfortunately, no decision is risk-free. It will be for you to decide which is the least risk. All we can do here is to help you understand some of the issues, so you can make an informed decision. For your information, major malformations occur 'spontaneously' in about 2–4% of all pregnancies, even if no drugs are taken. The main problem with medicines is termed 'teratogenicity', i.e. a medicine causing a malformation in the unborn child. A medicine causing teratogenicity is called a 'teratogen'. Since a baby has completed its main development between days 17 and 60 of the pregnancy (the so-called 'first trimester'), these first 2–16 weeks are the main concern. After that, there may be other problems, e.g. some medicines may cause slower growth. The infant may also be affected after birth, e.g. withdrawal effects are possible with some drugs.

If possible, the best option is to plan in advance. If you think you could become pregnant, discuss this with your doctor and it may be possible to switch to medicines thought to carry least risk, and take other risk-reducing steps, e.g. adjusting doses, taking vitamin supplements, etc. If you have just discovered you are pregnant, don't panic, but, if possible, seek advice from your GP within the next few days. He or she may also want to refer you on to someone with more specialist knowledge of your medicine.

Very few medicines have been shown to be completely safe in pregnancy, so no manufacturer or advisor can ever say any medicine is safe. They will usually advise not to take a medicine during pregnancy, unless the benefit is much greater than the risk. In the UK, there is the NTIS (National Teratology Information Service) which offers individual risk assessments. However, its advice should always be used to help you and your doctor decide what is the risk to you and your baby. There is a risk from taking the medicine and a risk should you stop a medicine, e.g. you might become ill again and need to go back on the medication. The advice offered here is just that—**advice**, but may give you some idea about the possible risks and what (at the time of writing) is known through the medical press.

It may be helpful to know that in the USA, the FDA (Federal Drug Administration) classifies medicines in pregnancy in five groups:

A =	Studies show no risk, so harm to the unborn child appears only a remote possibility
B =	Animal and human studies indicate a lack of risk, but are not fully conclusive
C =	Animal studies indicate a risk, but there is no safety date in humans
D =	A definite risk exists, but the benefit may outweigh the risk in some people
X =	The risk outweighs any possible benefit

Clozapine is classified as 'B'. The current information indicates that clozapine is not a major teratogen (i.e. a drug causing malformations). Some problems have, however, been reported and so you should seek personal advice from your GP, who may then, if necessary, seek further specialist advice.

Will I need a blood test?

Clozapine can upset the blood of about two or three in every hundred people taking it. It can reduce the number of white cells or neutrophils in the blood (neutropenia or agranulocytosis). This makes it much harder for your body to fight infections. You must, therefore, have regular blood tests for as long as you are taking this medicine.

Your doctor, pharmacist, or nurse will let you know when and where to have the tests. You will need a test before you start clozapine, then every week for the first 18 weeks, and every two weeks from then on. If you have been taking clozapine regularly for a year without any blood problems, it may be possible to change the blood tests to every four weeks. The blood is usually posted to a central laboratory, who return the results to the pharmacy and doctor.

You may also need extra blood tests if it is thought possible your blood is being affected. You must not miss these tests. Your doctor and pharmacist will not be able to let you have any more tablets if you do. Remember the rule: no blood, no tablets.

Can I drive while I am taking clozapine?

Clozapine can affect your driving in two ways. Firstly, you may feel drowsy and/or suffer from blurred vision when starting to take the drug. Secondly, clozapine can slow down your reactions or reflexes. This is especially true if you also have a dry mouth, blurred vision, or constipation (the so-called 'anticholinergic' side-effects). Until these effects wear off, or you know how your clozapine affects you, do not drive or operate machinery. You should take care, as clozapine may affect your reaction times or reflexes, even though you feel well.

It is advisable to let your insurance company know if you are taking clozapine. If you do not and you have an accident, it could affect your insurance cover.

If you are advised by your doctor not to drive, and continue to do so, the General Medical Council has advised doctors to inform the DVLA. The DVLA may then carry out an enquiry.

Treatments for 'side-effects'

Drug group: Anticholinergics or antimuscarinics

Drugs available	Brand name(s)	Forms available			
		Tablets	Capsules	Liquid	Injection
Benzhexol or trihexyphenidyl	Artane® Broflex®	✔		✔	
Benzatropine	Cogentin®	✔			✔
Biperiden	Akineton®	✔			
Orphenadrine	Disipal® Biorphen®	✔		✔	
Procyclidine	Kemadrin® Arpicolin®	✔		✔	

Benzhexol changed its name to trihexyphenidyl in 1998, but both names are still in use.

What are they used for?

Anticholinergics (or antimuscarinics) are most often used to help control some of the common side-effects that can occur with some antipsychotics (or neuroleptics), e.g. tremor, shaking, stiffness, or movement problems. These side-effects are known as the 'extrapyramidal' or 'Parkinsonian' side-effects. The anticholinergic drugs are very effective for this, but as these side-effects tend to wear off, you may not need to take an anticholinergic drug all the time. These drugs are also used to control the symptoms of Parkinson's disease itself.

How do they work?

Many of the symptoms of 'psychosis' are caused by over-activity of dopamine in the brain. Dopamine is a naturally occurring chemical messenger ('neurotransmitter') and antipsychotic drugs block its action. However, dopamine is also important in controlling muscle tone or tension. Unfortunately, the antipsychotic drugs also block the muscle controlling actions of dopamine and the tremor, stiffness, or movement problems mentioned above then occur due to this dopamine imbalance. In people who experience these side-effects, the effects of the transmitter 'acetylcholine' are greater than normal. Acetylcholine causes the muscles to become stiffer. Antimuscarinic or anticholinergic drugs reduce the action of acetylcholine, thus reducing these side-effects.

How should I take them?

Tablets:
The tablets should be swallowed with at least half a glass of water while sitting or standing. This is to make sure that they reach the stomach and do not stick in the throat.

Liquids:
Your pharmacist should give you a medicine spoon or oral syringe. Use it carefully to measure the correct amount. Ask your pharmacist for a medicine spoon if you do not have one.

When should I take them?

Take your medication as directed on the medicine label. These drugs can cause a dry mouth. Taking your medicine before food can help. They may also cause feelings of nausea or upset your stomach. If this happens it is best to take them after food as this will help. If you have a dry mouth and stomach upset, try taking your medicine after food and then sucking a peppermint, chewing gum, or drinking water to help your thirst and stop your mouth becoming dry.

Benzatropine ('Cogentin®') and biperiden ('Akineton®') can both make you feel sleepy, so if the instructions say to take them **once** a day this is usually better at bedtime. However, they are not sleeping tablets. Benzhexol/trihexyphenidyl , orphenadrine and procyclidine ('Kemadrin®') can have the opposite effect. You should avoid taking these at night if possible, as they may prevent you falling asleep.

How long will they take to work?

They start to work within an hour or so and the effect lasts for about 8–12 hours.

For how long will I need to keep taking them?

This should be discussed with your doctor as people's responses are different. Once the doses of your other drugs have settled down you may not need to take them regularly, only as necessary. If you are having a 'depot' injection you may only need these tablets for a few days after your injection.

Are they addictive?

These drugs are not addictive as such. There have been some reports of people 'abusing' them, but this is uncommon.

Can I stop taking them suddenly?

If you are taking them regularly, it is better not to stop taking them suddenly, as you symptoms may worsen. It is better to stop gradually and you should discuss this with your doctor. If you are only taking them 'when required' there is no problem.

What should I do if I forget to take them?

Start again as soon as you remember unless it is almost time for your next dose, then go on as before. Do not try to catch up by taking two or more doses at once, as you may experience more side-effects. You should tell your doctor about this at your next appointment. If you forget some doses and do not notice any difference, you may not need to take these at present. Talk about this with your doctor.

Will they make me drowsy?

These drugs may make you feel a little drowsy. You should not drive (see below) or operate machinery until you know how they affect you. You should take extra care, as they may affect your reaction times. Benzatropine ('Cogentin®') and biperiden ('Akineton®') can both make you feel sleepy, so if the instructions say to take them **once** a day, this is usually better at bedtime. However, they are not sleeping tablets. Benzhexol/trihexyphenidyl, orphenadrine and procyclidine ('Kemadrin®') can have the opposite effect. You should avoid taking these at night if possible, as they may prevent you from falling asleep.

What sort of side-effects might occur?

Side-effect	What happens	What to do about it
Common		
Blurred vision	Things look fuzzy and you cannot focus properly	Do not drive. See your doctor if you are worried. You will not need glasses
Dry mouth	Not enough saliva or spit	Suck boiled sweets or wine gums (but be careful if you are putting on weight). If it is still unpleasant, your doctor may be able to give you a mouth spray
Constipation	Feeling 'blocked up' inside. You cannot pass a motion	Make sure you eat enough fibre, bran, or fruit and that you are drinking enough fluid. Keep active and take plenty of exercise, e.g. walking. If this does not help, ask your doctor or pharmacist for a mild laxative
Rare		
Stomach upset	This includes nausea and diarrhoea (the runs)	If you feel like this for more than a week after starting the drug, tell your doctor. Taking it with food may help
Urine retention	Not much urine passed	Contact your doctor now
Dizziness	Feeling lightheaded and faint	Your dose may be too high, contact your doctor. Do not stand up too quickly. Try and lie down when you feel it coming on. Do not drive
Confusion	Your mind is all mixed up	Your dose may be too high; contact your doctor

Table adapted from UK Psychiatric Pharmacy Group leaflets, with kind permission (www.ukppg.org.uk)

Do not worry about this list of side-effects, as you may not experience any. There are other rare side-effects. If you develop any unusual symptoms, ask your doctor about these at your next appointment.

Will they cause weight gain?

It is not thought that any of the anticholinergics cause changes in weight. If you do start to have problems, tell your doctor at your next appointment and he/she can arrange for you to see a dietician for advice.

Will they affect my sex life?

Drugs can affect desire (libido), arousal (erection), and orgasmic ability. The anticholinergic drugs have not been reported to have a major adverse effect on these three stages. However, if this does happen, you should discuss it with your doctor, as a change in dose may help minimise the problem.

Can I drink alcohol while I am taking these drugs?

If you are taking benzatropine ('Cogentin®') or biperiden ('Akineton®'), you should avoid alcohol as it may make you feel sleepier. If you are taking one of the other anticholinergics and it makes you sleepy, you should also avoid alcohol as the alcohol may make this worse. This is particularly important if you need to drive or operate machinery, and you must seek advice on this.

Are there any foods or drinks that I should avoid?

You should have no problems with any food or drink other than alcohol (see above).

Will they affect my other medication?

You should have no problems if you take other medications, although a few have been recorded. Some other drugs, including the tricyclic antidepressants, MAOIs (antidepressants), the phenothiazine antipsychotics (e.g. chlorpromazine, thioridazine, 'Modecate®', trifluoperazine etc), and some antihistamines also have 'antimuscarinic' or 'anticholinergic' side-effects. If they are taken with an anticholinergic drug, the side-effects can worsen. Your doctor should know about these, but make sure your doctor knows about all the medicines you are taking. This does not necessarily mean the drugs cannot be used together, just that you may need to follow your doctor's instructions more carefully. In fact, anticholinergics are sometimes used to help treat the side-effects of phenothiazine antipsychotics.

Some other medicines, e.g. the painkiller co-proxamol ('Distalgesic'®) and some antihistamines can make you drowsy. When combined with your anticholinergic, this could make you even drowsier. You should tell your doctor before starting or stopping these, or any other drugs and consult your pharmacist before buying any medicines over the counter.

If I am taking a contraceptive pill, will this be affected?

It is not thought that the contraceptive pill is affected by these drugs.

What if I want to start a family or discover I'm pregnant?

It is important to consider that there will be a risk to you and your child from taking a medicine during pregnancy, but also a possible risk from stopping the medicine, e.g. suffering a relapse. Unfortunately, no decision is risk-free. It will be for you to decide which is the least risk. All we can do here is to help you understand some of the issues, so you can make an informed decision. For your information, major malformations occur 'spontaneously' in about 2–4% of all pregnancies, even if no drugs are taken. The main problem with medicines is termed 'teratogenicity', i.e. a medicine causing a malformation in the unborn child. A medicine causing teratogenicity is called a 'teratogen'. Since a baby has completed its main development between days 17 and 60 of the pregnancy (the so-called 'first trimester'), these first 2–16 weeks are the main concern. After that, there may be other problems, e.g. some medicines may cause slower growth. The infant may also be affected after birth, e.g. withdrawal effects are possible with some drugs.

If possible, the best option is to plan in advance. If you think you could become pregnant, discuss this with your doctor and it may be possible to switch to medicines thought to carry least risk, and take other risk-reducing steps, e.g. adjusting doses, taking vitamin supplements, etc. If you have just discovered you are pregnant, don't panic, but, if possible, seek advice from your GP within the next few days. He or she may also want to refer you on to someone with more specialist knowledge of your medicine.

Very few medicines have been shown to be completely safe in pregnancy, so no manufacturer or advisor can ever say any medicine is safe. They will usually advise not to take a medicine during pregnancy, unless the benefit is much greater than the risk. In the UK, there is the NTIS (National Teratology Information Service) which offers individual risk assessments. However, its advice should always be used to help you and your doctor decide what is the risk to you and your baby. There is a risk from taking the medicine and a risk should you stop a medicine, e.g. you might become ill again and need to go back on the medication. The advice offered here is just that—**advice**, but may give you some idea about the possible risks and what (at the time of writing) is known through the medical press.

It may be helpful to know that in the USA, the FDA (Federal Drug Administration) classifies medicines in pregnancy in five groups:

A =	Studies show no risk, so harm to the unborn child appears only a remote possibility
B =	Animal and human studies indicate a lack of risk, but are not fully conclusive
C =	Animal studies indicate a risk, but there is no safety date in humans
D =	A definite risk exists, but the benefit may outweigh the risk in some people
X =	The risk outweighs any possible benefit

The anticholinergics are all classified as 'C. There is no firm evidence of a teratogenic effect, but some problems have been reported and so you should seek personal advice from your GP, who may then, if necessary, seek further specialist advice.

Can I drive while I am taking them?

These drugs can affect your driving in two ways. You may feel drowsy and/or suffer from blurred vision when first taking any of them. Secondly, the drugs can slow down your reactions or reflexes. This is especially true if you also have a dry mouth, blurred vision, or constipation (the so-called 'anticholinergic side-effects'). Until these wear off or you know how your drug affects you, do not drive or operate machinery. You should take extra care, as they may affect your reaction times or reflexes, even though you feel well.

It is an offence to drive, to attempt to drive, or to be in charge of a vehicle when unfit through drugs.

If you are advised by your doctor not to drive, and continue to do so, the General Medical Council has advised doctors to inform the DVLA. The DVLA may then carry out an enquiry.

Caffeine

What is caffeine?

Caffeine is a central stimulant, i.e. it stimulates the brain. Caffeine is present in coffee, tea, cola drinks etc.

Is caffeine safe?

Drinking tea and coffee is a common social activity as well as being many people's main fluid intake during the day. Moderate amounts of caffeine, i.e. 250–500mg per day, are thought to be harmless unlike alcohol and nicotine, which have definite serious adverse effects. Indeed, it has been considered that most of the country would not operate properly without caffeine. However, higher amounts of caffeine can have noticeable unwanted effects.

What is caffeinism?

'Caffeinism' is the term used for people who are dependent upon caffeine, i.e. suffer toxic effects from having too much caffeine, take larger amounts, and need to keep drinking caffeine to function properly (this indicates a 'craving' for caffeine). 'Caffeinism' is thought to occur if your intake is above 600–750mg of caffeine per day. Drinking more than 1000mg per day is well into the toxic range. The US Olympic Committee considers caffeine a stimulant and has an upper limit for caffeine levels in the blood, above which an athlete 'fails a drug's test'.

People may drink large quantities of tea, coffee, and cola drinks to relieve thirst or dry mouth caused by the side-effects of drugs, such as some antidepressants and antipsychotics. Since headaches can occur when caffeine is stopped, drinking caffeine stops these headaches occurring.

What are the symptoms of caffeinism?

The symptoms of caffeinism can include: feelings of anxiety and nervousness, sleep disruption (especially difficulty in falling asleep), restlessness, irritability, diuresis (passing lots of water/urine), stomach complaints, tremulousness, palpitations, and arrhythmias (changed heart rate, especially a faster heartbeat). A dose of caffeine of 150mg at bedtime has been shown to have a marked effect on how long it takes to fall asleep, and reduces total sleep time, the quality of sleep, and REM (dreaming) periods. Caffeinism can make some illnesses, such as anxiety, more resistant to drug treatment. People who suffer from panic attacks may be more sensitive to the stimulant effects of caffeine.

To suddenly stop taking caffeine can cause problems. Withdrawal from even moderate amounts of caffeine can produce headaches (52%), anxiety (10%), rebound drowsiness, fatigue, and lethargy, with many other effects reported.

'Caffeinism' is considered a drug addiction and caffeine withdrawal syndrome is a documented psychiatric condition.

How do I know how much caffeine I take in a day?

You can work out your daily intake of caffeine using the following table:

Source of caffeine	Caffeine content	
	per 100ml	per container
Brewed coffee	55–85mg	140–210mg/mug
Instant coffee	35–45mg	85–110mg/mug
Brewed tea	25–55mg	85–110mg/mug
Cocoa	3mg	7mg/mug
Coca-Cola®	11mg	36mg/can
Pepsi-Cola®	7mg	22mg/can
Milk chocolate		around 22mg/100g
Dr Pepper®	11mg	36mg/can

*a mug is taken as being 250ml.

What should I do if my daily caffeine intake is too high?

Don't panic. If you are taking more than 600–750mg a day, you would probably feel better if you took less caffeine. However, since caffeinism can be considered a drug 'addiction', stopping caffeine suddenly is not advisable, as withdrawal effects (see previous page) are likely. If you are drinking too much caffeine, you should gradually reduce the amount to a safer level, preferably over several weeks. You can reduce your intake in many ways, e.g:

- use decaffeinated (or at least instant) coffee and/or tea sometimes
- avoid brewed coffee or strong tea
- either drink smaller volumes of coffee or tea, or make the drinks weaker
- mix decaffeinated coffee powder with ordinary coffee powder to make a lower caffeine drink
- drink caffeine drinks less often
- do not drink too many cola drinks, e.g. Coca-Cola®, Pepsi® etc.

A useful plan is to start with one or two decaffeinated drinks per day. Then increase this gradually, e.g. alternating decaffeinated drinks with ordinary caffeine-containing drinks or mixing decaffeinated coffee with ordinary coffee to make a drink of the same strength but lower in caffeine. Avoid taking caffeine drinks within two hours of going to bed.

Index

UNIVERSITIES AT MEDWAY LIBRARY